Ellen

Revolutionary Lives

Series Editors: Sarah Irving, University of Edinburgh;
Professor Paul Le Blanc, La Roche College, Pittsburgh

Revolutionary Lives is a series of short, critical biographies of radical figures from throughout history. The books are sympathetic but not sycophantic, and the intention is to present a balanced and, where necessary, critical evaluation of the individual's place in their political field, putting their actions and achievements in context and exploring issues raised by their lives, such as the use or rejection of violence, nationalism, or gender in political activism. While individuals are the subject of the books, their personal lives are dealt with lightly except insofar as they mesh with political concerns. The focus is on the contribution these revolutionaries made to history, an examination of how far they achieved their aims in improving the lives of the oppressed and exploited, and how they can continue to be an inspiration for many today.

Also available:

Salvador Allende:
Revolutionary Democrat
Victor Figueroa Clark

Hugo Chávez:
Socialist for the Twenty-first Century
Mike Gonzalez

Leila Khaled:
Icon of Palestinian Liberation
Sarah Irving

Jean Paul Marat:
Tribune of the French Revolution
Clifford D. Conner

Sylvia Pankhurst:
Suffragette, Socialist and Scourge of Empire
Katherine Connelly

Gerrard Winstanley:
The Digger's Life and Legacy
John Gurney

www.revolutionarylives.co.uk

Ellen Wilkinson

From Red Suffragist to Government Minister

Paula Bartley

PlutoPress
www.plutobooks.com

First published 2014 by Pluto Press
345 Archway Road, London N6 5AA

www.plutobooks.com

Distributed in the United States of America exclusively by
Palgrave Macmillan, a division of St. Martin's Press LLC,
175 Fifth Avenue, New York, NY 10010

British Library Cataloguing in Publication Data
A catalogue record for this book is available from the British Library

ISBN   978 0 7453 3238 3   Hardback
ISBN   978 0 7453 3237 6   Paperback
ISBN   978 1 7837 1016 4   PDF eBook
ISBN   978 1 7837 1018 8   Kindle eBook
ISBN   978 1 7837 1017 1   EPUB eBook

Library of Congress Cataloging in Publication Data applied for

This book is printed on paper suitable for recycling and made from fully managed
and sustained forest sources. Logging, pulping and manufacturing processes are
expected to conform to the environmental standards of the country of origin.

10   9   8   7   6   5   4   3   2   1

Typeset from disk by Stanford DTP Services, Northampton, England
Text design by Melanie Patrick
Simultaneously printed digitally by CPI Antony Rowe, Chippenham, UK and
Edwards Bros in the United States of America

For Réka and Dóra Dudley

Contents

List of Illustrations

Acknowledgements

I would like to thank a number of historians: Robert Pearce, who read and commented on an early draft of this book and whose advice, as ever, was invaluable; Lesley Hall, June Hanham, Karen Hunt, Sue Johnson, Christopher Knowles, Godfrey Lomas, Janis Lomas, Sue Morgan, Alison Ronan and Nicola Wilson for sharing their research and ideas with me; and Diane Atkinson, Maggie Andrews and Angela V. John who helped in a variety of useful ways. G.W. Jones patiently answered innumerable questions so a huge thanks to him too. I am grateful to other historians I have not referenced due to lack of space: a bibliography can be requested from drpaulabartley@outlook.com. Thanks also to Pluto Press and its editorial team for having faith in Ellen Wilkinson: in particular to David Castle and Sarah Irving for their support and guidance.

Historians are rightly indebted to archivists. I would like to thank Rob Whitfield, McMaster University, Canada; Elaine Moll, Hull History Centre; Professor Marion Shaw, literary executor of the Winifred Holtby archives; the Devon Record Office; Ian Rawes at the British Library; Guy Baxter and Danielle Mills at the University of Reading; Rayanne Byatt at the Coventry History Centre; Paul Taylor at the Birmingham Archives and Heritage Centre; Inderbir Bhullar at the Women's Library and all the archivists at the Bodleian, the National Archives and Middlesborough Central Library for their help. The Modern Record Centre at the University of Warwick was particularly obliging: Helen Ford even helped guide me through the complex business of copyright permissions. The reputation of Mancunians as friendly helpful people continues to thrive. It was always such a delight to visit any Manchester archive because everyone was so welcoming. Thank you to everyone at the Working Class Movement Library and to Jane Hodgkinson at the Manchester Archives and Local Studies Centre. Very extra special thanks to Darren Tredwell, at the People's History Museum, Manchester. His knowledge of Labour history and its archives is humungous and his help in my research was equally so. I spent many happy days at the USDAW office in Manchester. It was heartening to see a union in fine shape and whose attitude to any worker, including me, was supportive. Special thanks to George McLean, Emily Rowles, Alison Jeapes, Carol Bates, Tracey Gilbert and Angela Buckley for their generosity. Thanks also to Sid Gibson, Jarrow. I would also like to thank Phil Dunn at the People's History Museum, Ian White and Carol Darmouni at UNESCO, the TUC and Abby Gray at Getty for providing such great photographs of Ellen Wilkinson.

Cost would have made it difficult for me to have afforded to visit many of the archives. A generous grant, sponsored by Flora Fraser and Peter Soros, in affectionate memory of Elizabeth Longford, and administered by the Society of Authors enabled me to do archival research in London, Manchester, Newcastle and Liverpool. Thank you very, very much.

I would like to thank Clare Short who generously and openly shared with me what it was like to be a left-wing feminist in Parliament; and Mark Fisher, former MP for Stoke on Trent, who helped me understand life as a constituency MP for a working-class town blighted by unemployment. Thanks also to Rob and Jacqui Hamp, Teréz Kleisz, James and Kathy Stredder for their help, and to Diane Atkinson and Patrick Hughes for their amazing generosity.

My greatest thanks are to Jonathan Dudley who helped me with my research in Manchester, photographed material at Kew, accompanied me on very many research trips, read every word, deleted (nearly) every triplet and (nearly) every superfluous, redundant and often pointless adjective. The book is dedicated to younger members of our family.

Preface

One morning when it was pouring with rain, I took a taxi from Manchester Piccadilly railway station to USDAW[1] trade union headquarters and chatted to the cab driver. He asked me why I was in the city. When I told him I was writing a biography of Ellen Wilkinson his head swivelled round and he exclaimed 'Ellen Wilkinson? No way! My daughters used to go to the school named after her.' There was a brief pause until he said, 'Who was she?'

In her day 'Red Ellen' as she became known, was arguably the most famous, certainly the most outspoken, British woman politician. She was a fighter. A strong unionist and fierce left-wing socialist, she championed the poor and the vulnerable and was merciless in attacking the Conservatives for their complacency and self-interest. She developed strong feminist principles and for most of her life fought hard for equal rights for women. In October 1936, directly flouting Labour Party policy, she led 200 unemployed men on the Jarrow Crusade to London. Any form of political persecution was anathema to her and she fought against the growing Fascist menace throughout the 1930s, helping to acquit most of those accused of burning down the Reichstag and coordinating aid to the legitimate Spanish government. During the Second World War, Winston Churchill appointed her to a junior ministerial post where she took charge of shelter provision. By 1945, she was the most important woman in the Labour Party, co-authoring Labour's *Let us Face the Future*. When Labour won the post-war election and Clement Attlee set about forming his Cabinet, he pencilled in Ellen Wilkinson for Secretary of Health where she would have been responsible for the introduction of the National Health Service.[2] At her request, however, she was appointed Minister of Education – the first woman to hold this post. In between political activity, she wrote eight books, including two works of fiction.

'Red Ellen' may once have been famous but her name and reputation have faded from public consciousness. Recently, when a television documentary writer asked a female Labour MP how Ellen Wilkinson's career helped women in the Labour Party the MP replied 'Who is she?' Feminist historians are very aware that women who have made huge historically significant contributions can simply disappear, no ripple, no trace. To some extent historians, keepers of the bygone flame are responsible. Certainly, political historians who focus on male achievements have ignored Ellen. There are various biographies of her contemporaries in the Labour Party: Clement Attlee, Stafford Cripps, Herbert Morrison, Aneurin Bevan, Ernest Bevin and Harold Laski have all been the subject of historical attention. Feminist historians, who have analysed the absence of women from the political record and have sought to redress this imbalance, have also ignored her preferring to focus on the history of the under-privileged and of ordinary unknown women rather than one-time celebrities. Yet Ellen unquestionably deserves a place among the pantheon of Labour Party leaders since she played a major role during a crucial period in its history. I believe that Ellen Wilkinson not only witnessed but also helped create the twentieth-century breakthrough of the Labour Party into a governing party.

Thankfully, Ellen's importance is now being recognised if not written about in depth. She is mentioned in a number of history and cultural studies books, learned articles have been written about her, her character has appeared in plays and novels,[3] she has an entry in the *Oxford Dictionary of National Biography* and potted biographies of her life appear on many internet sites. She is even mentioned in the *Rough Guide to Britain*. Yet, when I began researching this book only one biography, Betty D. Vernon's *Ellen Wilkinson*, had been written.

A new biography is long overdue, especially since Ellen's life carries deep resonance for our times: Britain's economy is in recession with a government more committed to cut public spending than to create jobs or generate growth. A fierce critic of the inter-war Conservative governments, Ellen's life revolved around campaigns for social justice, educational reform, anti-capitalism and anti-imperialism, all of which aimed to change things for the better. In so many ways her political life and writing embodied the early years of the Labour, socialist, feminist and anti-imperialist movements and her participation made each of these stronger. As the figurehead of the feminist and the left in Parliament, she represented a distinct faction within the Labour Party and her life casts a fresh light on the often symbiotic, sometimes disjunctive, relationship between feminism and socialism in this period. Yet Ellen Wilkinson was no unthinking, slogan-shouting, banner-waving, doctrinal ideologue. Her politics stemmed from an intuitive empathy with the poor, the hungry, the weak and the dispossessed rather than a cool cerebral analysis of their economic dislocation.

Contemporaries of Ellen viewed her in various ways. The special combination of her tiny body, her coquettish personality and her hard-hitting socialist and feminist ideas appealed to many. She was only 4 feet 10 inches but she punched a good way above her height: 'though she be but little, she is fierce'.[4] Her friends and supporters believed she had an engaging charm and a vibrant personality – to them she was a courageous politician, a sincere and generous friend. She was thought to be a brilliant creature, 'a flame-like spirit giving life and light to thousands', with one of the quickest minds of the time. Careless of career she was rarely afraid to say the uncomfortable or the unsayable even though it may have cost her promotion. 'She had an instinct', said one colleague 'for the big thing'.[5] Many welcomed the freshness and passion that Ellen brought to politics and for a long time she was popular with the public: the affectionately teasing cartoons published about her and the sympathetic newspaper coverage she received provide evidence of this.

In contrast, others thought her an over-emotional self-publicist with the political attention of a butterfly. Sir James Erskine accused Ellen of being 'a tiny streak of superficial gusto ... as small in mind as you are in stature.'[6] Her enemies considered her too blinkered, intransigent, utopian and self-obsessed. Some believed that she acted like a precocious school girl, always showing off and wanting to be centre stage. Critics have pointed to her eclectic individuality and her tendency to pick up 'isms'. The radical Margaret Ashton thought Ellen Wilkinson's style a little too brusque and unpolished and maybe found her a bit too working class for comfort.

How does one reconcile these conflicting opinions? As a self-confessed 'heroine addict'[7] and shameless admirer of Ellen Wilkinson I am tempted to dismiss her critics as jealous, right-wing, unimaginative bureaucrats. Nonetheless, however much I may think that she was an inspirational figure, I have no desire to write a hagiography, nor present her as a one-dimensional figure with only a naïve understanding of politics. In this short book I cannot make an exhaustive study of her life so I therefore focus on what I believe were her key interests and achievements in the political sphere.

1

The Making of 'Red Ellen', 1891–1914

Ellen Wilkinson was born on 8 October 1891, in a two-up, two-down terraced house with a little back yard and an outside lavatory, at 41 Coral Street, Chorlton-on-Medlock. Until the nineteenth century, Chorlton was a small country village but industrialisation changed the area into a dirty and smoky adjunct of Manchester notorious for its back-to-back slum houses, its textile factories and its exploited workers. Only two classes mattered in Chorlton: the industrialists and the workers. Ellen was born into what she called the 'proletarian purple'.

She had two brothers and one sister: Annie, born in 1881, Richard in 1883, and Harold in 1899. Life was tough for the young family. When Ellen was born, her father was an insurance agent,[1] working as collector for a burial society. He was possibly under-employed at the time of her birth because her parents were unable to afford a competent midwife or doctor. Her mother had a difficult labour. At the time, there were no unemployment benefits, no free maternity care and certainly no child-welfare schemes to help the family. Ellen, who was a sickly child, must have strained the family finances: her mother endured a life of 'agonising suffering' and was usually too ill to work. In later life, Ellen commented that there was 'nothing in the least romantic about my youth'.[2]

The family lived in a grimy, overcrowded district of industrial Manchester but on her way to school Ellen walked past backstreet slums that were even worse. Engels had famously written earlier about this area as 'the most horrible spot, surrounded on all sides by tall factories, two hundred cottages, built chiefly back to back, in which live about four thousand human beings.'[3] Life had improved since

Engels' time but this working-class area remained sharply separated from the middle-class districts. At school, Ellen sat next to children who were hungry, badly clothed and ill-shod. She later criticised 'the inefficiency of commercialism, the waste, the extravagance, the poverty'[4] that she had seen in Manchester.

Her father, Richard, was a 'staunch trade-unionist' and Liberal Unionist. He had a simple political creed: 'I have pulled myself out of the gutter, why can't they?' was his unsympathetic reply to those who demanded his solidarity with the working class.[5] Ellen's indefatigable work ethic came straight from her father but she differed in one major respect: rather than condemn the poor for laziness she resolved to help them climb out of poverty.

Religion, in the form of Methodism, was a formative influence on the young Ellen. Her father and uncle were both local Methodist ministers and her brother Richard became one too. Her training in public speaking began early: she recalled repeating sermons to a grandmother too ill to attend chapel, reciting poems at the Band of Hope, making speeches dressed as a Chinese or an Indian girl at the missionary meetings and talking in school debates. It was an early training for complete unselfconsciousness on a public platform and a safe place to practise and refine her gifts as an orator. More importantly, in the opinion of Ellen and others, the 'Fatherhood of God and the Brotherhood of Man' was an assertion of equality which the next generation found in socialism. These basic Christian principles of social justice and egalitarianism undoubtedly shaped her later socialist compassion. Some years on, Ellen recalled that her Methodism was not 'narrowly religious' but had a political edge. It was here that she first learned of the Congo atrocities, the colonisation of Ireland and India and sweated labour at home.[6] Sermons about such topics influenced a young impressionable girl, and maybe taught Ellen to fight for international justice. Certainly, she belonged to the old tradition of Christian Socialism, and appropriated the millenarian, emotional, sentimental rhetoric of Methodism and, some might argue, its tendency towards fanaticism. Ellen's later speeches at street meetings, on upturned package cases and other hastily constructed platforms, were as fervent and passionate as a Methodist revivalist meeting. Moreover, like all good religious evangelists her beliefs usually tended to be definite.

Ellen's education deepened her sense of injustice. In 1902, aged eleven, she attended the Ardwick Higher Elementary School near her home in Coral Street. Here she became impatient with the 'vast educational sausage factory' of education: she was bored and loathed the often sadistic behaviour of her teachers. 'What remains with me', she stated in an autobiographical sketch, 'is a vivid hatred of those schools'. She swore that if appointed to the Board of Education, her first job would be to 'tackle the problem of the type of teaching in elementary schools'. After this school, she put up with 'two horrid unmanageable years' at Stretford Road Secondary school for girls. Fortunately, her father Richard who had had no formal education was an autodidact who encouraged Ellen to be the same. He took his young daughter to lectures and gave her books by authors such as Aldous Huxley and Charles Darwin, all the while encouraging Ellen in an unshakeable self-confidence.

Ellen was clever but at the time there were few educational and professional opportunities for women, especially from working-class backgrounds. Teaching, the most obvious career choice for intelligent girls, involved either a degree course at a university, a two-year course at a teacher training college or, for those less financially secure, a combination of pupil teaching and training college. At the age of 16, Ellen enrolled at the Manchester Pupil Teacher's Centre. Her keen intelligence and outgoing personality made her stand out. Two teachers in particular recognised her potential and encouraged her to write stories and articles for the school magazine and to speak in public on the political issues of the day. In Ellen's opinion, her real education began when she was asked to stand as a socialist candidate in mock elections. During her research she read Robert Blatchford and later recalled that his *Britain for the British* and *Merrie England* made her a convinced socialist. She defended her new beliefs to an audience of about 500 16- to 18-year-olds – and dealt effectively with her first group of hecklers.

After her experiences in the mock election Ellen wanted to enter that 'magic sphere of politics'. She dressed up in her Sunday best and went along to her first Independent Labour Party branch meeting at

Longsight. This 16-year-old, tiny, unaccompanied young woman was the first to arrive at the meeting and witnessed a few men strolling in. She was completely baffled by the shorthand used by those at the meeting: acronyms such as the ASRS, the ASLE, and the SDF which were meaningless to a young and still politically naïve teenager. Ellen slipped away from the meeting 'feeling that if this were politics there seemed to be little room for me'. Fortunately she overcame her nerves and was persuaded to go to another, bigger meeting, at the Free Trade Hall.

This meeting was decisive. Once again, the very excited Ellen was one of the first to arrive and walked straight to the front row. A number of men spoke but her attention centred on a 'small slim woman, in a plain woollen frock of a soft blue, her hair simply coiled into her neck': Katherine Bruce Glasier, a prominent figure in the labour movement. Glasier, who was not much taller than Wilkinson, was the embodiment of her dream for a political life. Ellen later wrote that 'to stand on the platform of the Free Trade Hall, to be able to sway a great crowd as she swayed it, to be able to make people work to make life better, to remove slums and underfeeding and misery … that seemed the highest destiny any woman could ever hope for.'

Katherine Glasier's speeches, considered to be highly emotional, with an ethically Christian 'Come-unto-Jesus' style of socialism, no doubt appealed to young Ellen Wilkinson's Methodist spirit.[7] She wanted to be like her heroine. At the end of the meeting, she met Glasier who urged her to 'come out and speak at our meetings. We need young women for Socialism.' But Ellen felt both inspired and depressed: on the one hand she had found a cause in which she believed, on the other hand she was deeply conscious that, as a young woman, she could not advance socialism herself. 'Only you fellows' she said bitterly, 'will be able to go to Parliament and do the job, and they won't even let me vote for it.' She knew at the time, she later said, that the Labour Party existed to get men into an all-male Parliament for which only men could vote. Nevertheless, in 1907, in spite of her reservations Ellen joined the Longsight Independent Labour Party and remained a member until it disaffiliated from the Labour Party. Many years later, she sent Glasier a copy of *Myself When Young*, in which she had written an autobiographical sketch.

It included a warm tribute to her idol. Ellen always insisted that it was Katherine Glasier who 'brought me into the Socialist movement. What a very great soul she is. It always made me humble to think of her indomitable courage.'[8]

Meanwhile, Ellen had to study and learn to teach. She loved the education offered at the college but hated her weekly two-and-a-half days teaching experience, largely because of the way in which teachers treated their young charges. She recalled her first day at school assembly when a 'vindictive old cat, grey-haired and spinsterish' slapped one pupil who was not praying and insisted that he 'Say Gentle Jesus, you little nuisance, say Gentle Jesus'. In later years, she admitted that she was psychologically unable to visit an elementary school when she was on the Education Committee of the Manchester City Council because of these earlier experiences.

In 1910, aged 19, Ellen won the Jones Open History Scholarship to Manchester University. Now she began to 'live life to the full, as I had always dreamed of living it ... books unlimited, lots of friends, interesting lectures, stimulus of team work'. It was here that she learned the research skills and the clear analytical, factually accurate writing she was to use in Committees and other official forums. Yet even so, Ellen thought the History syllabus, dominated by high politics, war and diplomacy, dull: she wanted to learn how ordinary women and men had lived.

It was here that she developed her political voice. Ellen worked hard on a range of projects, all the time testing and refining her emerging beliefs: she helped found the University Socialist Federation and later became vice-chair;[9] she organised meetings such as those addressed by the radical trade unionist and feminist Mary McArthur; in 1912 she joined the Manchester Society for Women's Suffrage (MSWS), and ran the local branch of the Fabian Society; in 1913 she joined the Tyldesley branch of the Women's Labour League; and she graduated. Ellen was thought capable of gaining a first class degree but she had concentrated more on her politics than her studies and was awarded a second. She couldn't wait to put her ideas into practice. The period just before the First World War is often seen as a revolutionary time when socialists, feminists, trade unionists and other rebels fought to change a system deemed to disadvantage the many. Ellen Wilkinson,

Figure 1.1 Ellen in her graduation gown.
(People's History Museum, Manchester)

along with a number of her more radical contemporaries, was ready to overturn the status quo.

Her time at Manchester University made it possible for Ellen to abandon the teaching she disliked and train for her much-desired political career. In July 1913, now aged 21, she began to achieve her ambition when the MSWS,[10] a branch of the suffragist National Union of Women's Suffrage Societies (NUWSS), appointed her 'assistant organiser in training' at a salary of two guineas a week, a decent wage for a young woman just out of university. She joined the staff of the MSWS just in time to help organise the July Suffrage Pilgrimage where women from all over the country walked to Hyde Park, London, to publicise women's suffrage. Ellen spoke at open-air meetings in Manchester and nearby towns advertising the Pilgrimage, all the time learning how to capture the attention of sometimes reluctant audiences. On 6 July 1913, as a send-off to the pilgrims, a procession of over 600 supporters marched from Albert Square, Manchester to Stockport, with women university students and graduates like Ellen encouraged to wear their caps and gowns.[11]

It may seem surprising that the fiery and rebellious Ellen joined the peaceful, constitutional suffragists rather than the window-breaking, arsonist and militant suffragettes. Temperamentally she seemed more suited to suffragette methods yet it was highly unlikely that a young working-class woman from a respectable Methodist family would take part in violent action. Perhaps more importantly, in 1912 the Labour Party promised to support votes for women and suffragists pledged to help them get elected; in contrast suffragettes eschewed any affiliation to any political party. Her MSWS job allowed Ellen to combine her emerging feminism and socialism when she was given the job of liaising with the Labour Party.[12] Ellen, a strong Labour supporter, had not only found her natural home but was learning fund-raising tactics, organisational skills, campaign tactics and about the inner workings of a constituency. She helped set up a Suffrage and Labour Club in Ancoats which in the first three months of its life recruited 70 members, raising funds by organising jumble sales and whist drives.[13] The MSWS believed that 'the organisation of these clubs is one of the distinctive features of the work of the Manchester Society and they have done much to popularise the question of women's suffrage.'[14] The Labour Party, impressed by Miss Wilkinson's political acumen, asked her to sit on a Committee set up to get Labour candidates into Parliament.[15]

Ellen spoke at countless meetings, organised the heckling of MPs opposed to votes for women and distributed bucket-loads of leaflets. Oratory, debate and counter-attack are at the heart of politics and it was here that she developed her skills in coping with hostile audiences. She became an exceedingly able speaker and was particularly good at open-air meetings. Stella Davies, a family friend, spoke of how Ellen often faced intimidating crowds. Once when Ellen was standing on an open lorry campaigning for Votes for Women, she was greeted by yells and cat-calls from an angry male crowd who threw stones at her, shouting at the diminutive red-head: 'Go home, Carrots, and darn the stockings.' Undeterred, she carried on.

Ellen was a minor figure in the MSWS but she was learning fast. As a paid suffrage worker she read the suffragist newspaper, *The Common Cause*, listened to suffrage speakers, discussed suffragist aims and strategy, gained experience in public speaking and developed organisational skills. While helping the Labour Party, Ellen learned that getting elected was a long-term process and that constituencies needed to be 'nursed' by candidates and their supporters. All the time she was developing her understanding of the craft of politics.

On 4 August 1914, Britain declared war on Germany. In Ellen's view, the war was unjustifiable and people should oppose it. She judged it an imperialist war fought over territorial rights: Great Britain which had colonised large parts of the world, particularly in Africa, was challenged by Germany who wanted its own 'place in the sun'. War, she maintained, meant millions of workers killing each other in the interests of their bosses. These were brave, and somewhat naïve, statements as a wave of nationalism swept the country: men flocked to enlist and jingoism was rife.

Ellen's employer, the NUWSS, was bitterly divided over the war: some members wholeheartedly supported the war effort; others were ambivalent; and still others were unwilling to countenance war in any shape or form. Some became arch-imperialists. The suffragette leader, Emmeline Pankhurst, remarked that there was no point in continuing to fight for the vote when there might be no country to vote in; the suffragist leader, Millicent Fawcett, approved of these sentiments and declared: 'Women, your country needs you.' Eventually these disagreements led to an acrimonious break-up of the NUWSS when its leaders refused to recognise the legitimacy of an international peace conference for women held at The Hague. In the end all the national NUWSS executive, apart from Millicent Fawcett and the Treasurer, resigned and in September 1915 formed the British section of the Women's International League for Peace and Freedom. The situation in Manchester, where she worked, was equally fraught. Virtually the whole of the NUWSS branch, including Ellen, transferred their allegiance to the new organisation.

The MSWS unanimously agreed to stop suffrage activity to help 'sufferers from the economic and industrial dislocation caused by the war'.[16] This was potentially disastrous for Ellen. Unlike some of the women in the Manchester NUWSS, she was neither wealthy nor well-connected and needed to find paid work. Fortunately, the MSWS was keen to keep on its suffrage staff and found her a job in Stockport helping to organise voluntary help for the relief of distress caused by war.[17] Once in post, her natural appetite for hard work resurfaced and her organising skills were once more evident. Ellen first wrote to all the various religious and political organisations asking them to help collect money for relief work. The two staple trades of Stockport, cotton and knitting, collapsed when war broke out so, conscious of the region's high female unemployment, she commandeered a large room, borrowed machines and tables, appealed in the Press for materials and second-hand clothing and opened a sewing room. Soon the workshop employed 150 women.[18]

Ellen was later appointed Honorary Secretary to the Manchester branch of the Women's Emergency Corps (WEC).[19] The WEC was started two days after the declaration of war with a two-fold aim: to find a 'suitable outlet for the many offers of help from women of all classes and to provide jobs for those thrown out of work by war'.[20] Ellen must have felt out of place since the WEC 'bustled with suffragettes, fashionable actresses, a couple of duchesses and a marchioness, and a handful of lady novelists' as well as a number of countesses and ladies.[21] Although she welcomed the post since it gave her 'time to find something else',[22] she began to look for a job more suited to her political ambitions.

2

The First World War and its Aftermath, 1914–24

In July 1915, now aged 23, Ellen Wilkinson found a job suited to her politics, ideals and temperament: she became a national organiser for the Amalgamated Union of Co-operative Employees, (AUCE), with special responsibility for organising women shop assistants and factory workers. She was an unusual appointment in that she had never worked in a Co-op store nor been active as a grassroots union shop steward. Unusual too in that she had a university degree. However, from now on, the AUCE would form an important part of Ellen's life. It would further her political education, help her form alliances within the labour movement, consolidate her organisational skills, finance her politics and make it possible for her to become an MP. Importantly, it was here that Ellen's long-lasting friendship with her colleague and future union president, John Jagger, was forged. They were to remain close until Jagger died in a motorbike crash during the Second World War.

The AUCE was an ideal job. Ellen was paid a decent salary and could claim for travel costs and other expenses: for example in the month of November 1918 she was paid a wage of £25 and claimed £10 1s 4d in travel and £10 7s 0d for expenses.[1] She threw herself into the union's battles with all the daring of her youth. The AUCE journal, *The New Dawn*, later declared that:

> [I]t would be true to say that there has scarcely ever been a fight … in which she has not taken a prominent part. Her strong points are economics, oratory and organisation (she'll organise the angels whenever she gets to heaven) and her weak ones are mathematics and finance. (She is always in a chronic state of bankruptcy). She

works night and day during a crisis and plays like a school-girl when work is done.[2]

In fact Ellen was seen to put so much unbounded energy into the AUCE disputes that the President was 'inclined to wonder whether a great deal of the militancy was not of her creating'.[3]

The First World War turned equal pay into a major issue. 'Women of brains and initiative, with responsible and arduous posts', Ellen complained, 'are still hampered by that strong tradition that a woman's wages are practically settled for ever when she has become twenty-one, and that however important a woman's work may be, she must be considered as assistant to some male manager'.[4] The majority of women, from cotton factory weavers through to Civil Service mandarins, received less pay than their male colleagues because men were thought to be physically stronger, did not leave on marriage and had greater family responsibilities. Consequently when women replaced the men who were called up to fight, employers wanted to pay them less. Ellen however insisted 'the rate for the job, not the sex of the worker' should be the only criterion for pay.[5] By late 1916 she had negotiated male rates of pay for women in 57 different societies across the United Kingdom.[6]

Some of Ellen's time was spent on mundane work, doing the painstaking task of recruiting members, negotiating wages and conditions. She channelled a lot of her energy in improving the lives of laundry workers. Everyday conditions in the trade were hazardous. Burns were common. Even without the dangers, laundry work was hot, back-breaking, exhausting work, the atmosphere was stiflingly thick with steam or gas, and the floors were usually swimming in water. In one of her first short stories entitled *Steam and Starvation* published in her union journal, she wrote, 'The ironers bending over gas irons and collar machines felt the fumes rise in their faces. Aching heads and aching backs, and always behind them the shrill, nagging voice of the fore-women saying "Stick at it girls, the first delivery goes in an hour. Stop talking there".'[7] Laundry workers were, like shop assistants, notoriously difficult to organise since the industry was split into a large number of small, often home-based, units. Painstakingly and carefully Ellen and the newly established Joint Laundry Board[8] improved wages and conditions for laundry workers in a number of large towns. Finally, after considerable negotiation, she helped hammer out a national programme of wages and conditions of labour for all the laundries affiliated to the Co-operative Society.[9]

In July 1915, the Munitions of War Act forbade strikes and made arbitration compulsory in all industries involved in war work. The firebrand Ellen now had to negotiate with the government as well as employers. It is sometimes (wrongly) assumed that there were hardly any strikes in the First World War because of government restrictions, but in fact there were strikes in the mines, on the Clyde and a fair few in the AUCE. The strikes in which Ellen played a part were centred upon pay and conditions but they were also – importantly – about the right of the AUCE to unionise. When she began her job, the AUCE mainly organised shop assistants in the Co-operative stores and had little desire to recruit outside it. However, Co-op societies employed a variety of crafts people, from bacon curers to bakers, from cooks to carters, from soap makers to shoe-repairers, hardly any of whom were unionised. Only very few craftspeople worked in each individual Co-op so the Craft Unions, which they should have joined, did not bother to recruit them. Yet when these workers approached the sympathetic AUCE, some of the Craft Unions objected and tried to prevent them joining. Indeed, before the 1939 Bridlington Agreement, unions were regularly accused of poaching each other's members and inter-union conflict was common.

In autumn 1916, Ellen was involved in the first of the bitter fratricidal conflicts between her union, the Co-operative Society and the Craft Unions. The battle was sparked off when the Plymouth Co-operative Society refused to increase the pay of its workers. Ellen thought that a strike might occur and so, with her usual commitment and dedication, spent her summer holiday near Plymouth so that she could be ready for 'any eventualities'.[10] When the strike began on 9 September 1916 most of the employees downed tools, closed their tills and shut up their shops. Ellen and the other organisers were soon in the thick of it, holding meetings, speaking to strikers and trying to negotiate with the Co-op. They looked set to win until the Craft Unions encouraged their own union members to remain at work. 'Whatever may be the nature of the quarrels between one union and another', she complained, 'our members are looking with abhorrence at this dastardly business of black-legging'.[11] The conflict between the three groups led to the MP for Plymouth, Waldorf Astor, and his wife, Nancy, taking an interest. Ellen and the other organisers spent nearly two hours with the Astors, who were allegedly sympathetic to the need for better wages.[12] Eleven weeks later, the AUCE admitted defeat and the strikers were forced into arbitration. The AUCE also lost members: in May 1918 the Plymouth branch decreased to 291 members after a high of nearly 800 at the time of the strike.[13]

The Plymouth strike was the start of several internecine conflicts between the Co-operative Society, the AUCE and the Craft Unions. In July 1918, Ellen became embroiled in one of the nastiest, this time at the printing works at Longsight, Manchester. It began as a strike for better wages before seguing into another battle over the right of the AUCE to recruit and negotiate. Once again, the Craft Unions tried to undermine the AUCE's attempt to obtain better pay and working conditions.[14] Finally, the government intervened, censured the AUCE and insisted that members return to work.[15] It was yet another humiliating defeat for Ellen and the AUCE.

On 11 November 1918, the First World War ended. Just over a month later Ellen lost her job largely as a result of her perceived mismanagement of the Longsight strike. The Executive pronounced that 'Miss E C Wilkinson be dismissed from the service of the Union, her engagement to terminate on February 8th, 1919'[16] and advertised for a new woman organiser. Branches, groups and individuals all sent letters of protest, a deputation of union representatives asked for an unconditional withdrawal of notice, and a Special Delegate Meeting challenged the right of the Executive Council to dismiss Ellen.[17] In the end a compromise was reached. Ellen apologised for her role in the strike and the union decided 'that Miss Wilkinson's apology be accepted, and that she be reinstated'.[18]

During the war Ellen was elected to the Standing Joint Committee of Industrial Women's Organisations (SJC), an organisation which acted as the advisory body to the Labour Party on women's questions.[19] By February 1923 she was on the Executive, along with Susan Lawrence and Marion Phillips.[20] In July 1925 she was chair.

Ellen Wilkinson was now on the way to becoming a key figure in the Labour Party.

Armistice and its Aftermath

After the war many leading figures (such as Emmeline Pankhurst) lost their political drive and faded into obscurity. Ellen, on the other hand, quickly emerged as a talented young politician. She continued to hone her organising skills in the trade union movement, helped to found the Communist Party, campaigned for peace and promoted the rights of women. In the early 1920s she belonged to a number of different, and often competing, political groups, such as the Communist Party, the Independent Labour Party, the Fabians and the Labour Party. It may seem odd that Ellen belonged to so many groups but she was still trying out the politics which would suit her best. Moreover, at the time politics was a little more fluid – there was less allegiance to just one party and it was common for socialists to belong to more than one national organisation

In June 1919, Ellen had a change of job within her union.[21] She switched to Central Office and became part of a nucleus of trained specialists, advisors, investigators, negotiators and speakers acting in a national capacity at government inquiries, arbitrations, on Trade Boards and other bodies. It was a promotion of sorts. Initially the post-war economy was relatively buoyant so she was able to improve the wages and conditions in many sweated trades. In June 1919, Ellen and the union members of the Trade Board successfully negotiated a 48-hour week for laundry workers and an improved minimum wage. This boom period was not to last. When the economy collapsed in 1921, largely because of industrial decline, Ellen spent the next few years fighting to prevent wage cuts and deteriorating working conditions. In almost every branch of the union there were wage reductions, in some cases twice in a year. There was also a heavy loss of female members. In 1921 there were 72,267 women members of AUCE but a year later this had almost halved to 36,902. Ellen blamed this 'on the way that the women's interests have been handled by some of the Unions during the last three years'[22] but her judgement was awry – women left the union because they lost their jobs when men returned from the war. Meanwhile the AUCE, hoping to halt the dramatic decline in membership, amalgamated with the Warehouse Workers Union to form the National Union of Distributive and Allied Workers (NUDAW).

Ellen continued to be committed to defending women's rights. It was a measure of her growing reputation that she was appointed chair of the Workers' Side of the Laundry Trades Boards and a member of the Laundry, Corset, Dressmaking and Millinery Trades Boards. One of her many outstanding achievements was to be a witness to the Cave Select Committee set up in 1922 to examine wages in the Distributive and Laundry Trades. Ellen, trained as an historian, gathered her evidence impeccably, organising a four-day conference of witnesses to make sure her facts were accurate.[23] She gave evidence on 22 December and 10 January, compiling 'a case bristling with fighting facts', and made an immense impression by her description of conditions and the low wages associated with laundry work. She was examined for well over two hours and her evidence ran to 20 pages.[24] Her union colleague, Wright Robinson, thought her 'piquant, quite decided, and the Committee were probably amused that such large opinions should be associated with such small stature. All the same they respected her greatly. She gave her evidence well, adopting the University manner, and turning both words and sentences carefully.'[25]

In other situations, where action rather than analysis was called for, Ellen was less measured. In May 1923, she was embroiled in a long drawn-out strike when the Co-op directors imposed a series of wage cuts, mostly affecting its female staff. From 1922, there was a deflationary economy and many workers had to accept a wage reduction but Ellen was determined to protect the wages of Co-op workers. She was once again in her element, challenging the Co-op directors, rushing around the country gaining support, speaking to striking workers. Wright Robinson, now less enamoured with Wilkinson and jealous of her growing reputation, wrote in his diary that 'Ellen Wilkinson and Jagger in combination appear to stick at nothing that stands in their way. Either will lie roundly, or ignore or gloss over factors which would tell against the plan for the moment, with the result that not one of us believes anything they say, or trust any move they make.' In his view, the two union officials had used their position in the union to bring the Co-op workers out on strike when the dispute should have gone to arbitration. 'With Jagger in command Ellen W had a free hand and conducted a publicity campaign, mostly abuse of the directors, totally unreliable as to the truth and vixenish and confusing rather than clever or convincing.' Wright Robinson believed that Jagger 'is a big personal force in the clutches of a little vulgar clever and unscrupulous woman'.[26] This time the strike ended in a muted victory when Wilkinson, Jagger and NUDAW secured the rights of the union to organise. Unfortunately, when the dispute was submitted to arbitration the wage cuts were upheld.[27]

Ellen was quick to indict the blatant sexism of male trade unionists for their defeat and believed that union attitudes were the main reason why women did not join. 'If we want women in the trade union movement,' she urged

> we have to stand up for them and give equal treatment ... You found men fighting not for decent rates for the women, but against the women with the result that women regarded their employers as better able to look after their interests than the trade unions ... Remember, it was left to an arbitration court, consisting wholly of working men Trade Unionists, and co-operatives, to give the largest reduction in women's wages that has ever been given by any single court of arbitration.[28]

She was referring to the Co-operative strike of 1923.

Communism and Pacifism

In October 1917, the Bolsheviks seized power and attempted to create a socialist state in Russia. Like many on the left, Ellen was swept away by the Russian revolution and became excited by the possibility of socialism in the United Kingdom. Her union sent fraternal greetings to Russia 'congratulating them on their magnificent victory for the cause of freedom and justice'.[29] One New Year's Eve, standing on a balcony in Paris with the revolutionary socialist Rajani Palme Dutt, 'while the crowd danced below in the square, the romance of the revolution temporarily overcame her ... and by the morning she had promised to join the future Communist Party when it would be formed in Britain'.[30]

The Communist Party of Great Britain was created at a conference in the summer of 1920. It condemned parliamentary government as an 'instrument of capitalist domination' and welcomed the Soviet form of government. The newly formed party chose Ellen to be one of a special commission of five members to formulate a Programme of Action. Contradictorily, the British Communist Party, encouraged by Lenin and the Bolsheviks, also tried to affiliate to the Labour Party in order to redirect its policy. However since the Labour leadership regarded communism as ideologically incompatible with parliamentary democracy this was an unrealistic hope. Communists, the Labour Party Executive maintained, wanted a 'Dictatorship of the Proletariat' by armed revolution. At the 1921 Labour Party conference, the delegates voted by 4,115,000 to 224,000 not to affiliate to the Communist Party and reaffirmed this decision over the next three years. Ellen wavered between the Communist Party and the Labour Party until forced to make a choice. In future, the strained relationship between the two groups would cause her all sorts of practical and ideological difficulties.

The Soviet Union paid a stipend to its British comrades and helped subsidise the Communist Party in England. There is no evidence that Ellen received regular payments but the Soviets did give her and Harry Pollitt, later to become General Secretary of the British Communist Party, letters of credit worth £500 to travel first class to the Congress of the Red Trade Union International in Moscow.[31] Here she met Trotsky, then Soviet Minister of Defence, who 'wore a shabby khaki shirt and translated his own Russian speeches into three other languages when the translation staff got hopelessly overworked'.[32] She kept in contact with Trotsky after the conference, writing to him, trying to get permission for him to come to Britain when he was deported from the Soviet Union[33] and sending him copies of Hansard and other parliamentary papers when he was in exile near Istanbul.[34] Ellen also encountered some of the leading women revolutionaries such as Nadezhda Krupskaya and Alexandra Kollontai, commenting that Krupskaya's 'magnificent speech' was the best in the debate.

In 1921, in order to further the revolutionary cause, Ellen helped found the Red International of Labour Unions, commonly known as the Profintern, an international body established with the help of the Soviets' representative, Grigory Zinoviev, and firmly linked to the Soviet Communist International. The Red International aimed to create a revolutionary Labour Union to wage class war and ensure the triumph of the working class. Ellen certainly believed that trade unions could act as a force for revolutionary change. Direct action, she declared, should be the basis of all trade union tactics, 'not merely strikes but boycotts, street demonstrations, violent opposition to the conveyance of goods to or from blackleg enterprises ... to prepare workers for social revolution and the dictatorship of the proletariat ... the ability to stop transport and the extraction of coal, being one of the most powerful weapons in the hands of the workers.' In the heady revolutionary days of post-war Russia it was believed that world revolution was just around the corner. Ellen wrote 'there is but one aim for us – the overthrow of world capitalism. To secure this there can only be one army, the International of the World Proletariat.'[35]

Many British people, including large numbers of trade unionists, disliked revolutionary politics and believed that the newly created Soviet Union was a disaster. In an article entitled 'Help Russia', Ellen complained that newspapers misinformed their readers: poor Russia, she claimed, had indeed been devastated by war, drought and famine but was 'working out a great experiment in government that the world cannot afford to lose. From the depths of age-long oppression she struggled to the light in 1917'.[36] Russia, she believed, could only be successful if the world was socialist and she urged the working class to send help to Russia and to foment revolution in Britain. Ellen Wilkinson, echoing Lenin and the other Bolshevik leaders, believed that socialism could not happen just in one country. In order for socialism to be successful it must be international: 'it is no more possible to have a Communist Russia in a capitalist world,' Ellen commented, 'than to have a Communist Manchester in a Capitalist Britain.'[37]

As a feminist, Ellen was deeply interested in the position of women in the new Soviet Republic. In one of the first articles to be published in the newly created *Communist Review* she praised the Bolsheviks for their feminist principles. In her view, women in Russia were given the most complete freedom that legislation could bestow: the right to vote for and to fill any office; the right to equal pay and equal rations; the right to seek an abortion. She praised Russia too for ensuring its 'illegitimate' children carried no social or legal stigma, and paid tribute to the revolutionary zeal of the Bolsheviks in promoting the emancipation of women. Sometimes she used language now considered objectionable. 'The problem of the Mohammedan women, and the enclosed women of the various Eastern races,' she said, 'has been tackled by the Women's Secretariat ... the Eastern women with minds as veiled as their faces meeting, often for the first time, the revolutionary women, eager and emancipated, whose restless, searching minds would accept no tradition ... strong resolutions passed in favour of the emancipation of Moslem women and the ending of polygamy.'[38] What Muslim women thought of their enforced freedom was not recorded.

In Ellen's opinion, Russian women had taken the lead in advancing the emancipation of women workers. She criticised countries like the United Kingdom where women were supposedly liberated. 'What has really happened', she maintained, 'is that a few rich women have used their working class sisters to get rid of bonds that were irksome to the ladies, who, with the spoil of victory, then retired into the ranks of capitalism.'[39] Real freedom, Ellen insisted, meant revolution. She continually stressed that the wrongs of women as a sex were closely related to the wrongs of the exploited masses. Ellen may have been well-intentioned but she was mythologising Soviet Russia as, at the time, civil war was raging and little other than paper reforms existed.

Ellen joined peace organisations but she was not a pacifist in the conventional sense, since her support for peace was premised on anti-imperialism rather than being anti-war per se. There were tensions between those who believed in pacifism and those who were anti-imperialist and this surfaced most strongly at the end of the war. At the first meeting of the Women's International League for Peace and Freedom (WILPF) in 1919 delegates disagreed over the use of force. At one end of the peace spectrum lay those who believed in absolute pacifism; at the other end were those who divided the use of armed force into unjustifiable and justifiable, condemning armed

Figure 2.1 Women's International League for Peace and Freedom, Zurich, 1919 (Ellen is second left, first row). (TUC History Online)

force used by capitalists but supporting armed struggle to promote socialism.[40] It is said that Ellen, who attended the conference, was so firmly in the latter camp that a fellow Labour Party member asked her to tone down her revolutionary zeal.[41] Unfortunately, we have no record of any revolutionary speeches made by her. She spoke a number of times: on self-government in industry, on self-government in schools, on increasing the numbers serving on particular committees and proposing that women 'take a new stand for the new times and not let ourselves be frightened by the old story that what is ideal is unpractical. We maintain that we shall be able to find the practical way to realise our ideal'.[42] Her most militant proposal echoed the Balfour Declaration when it demanded

> that in accord with the right of self-determination … perfect equal right of the Jews in all countries; … international protection of the Jew and all national minorities against physical persecutions and economical oppressions; equal rights for the Jews with regard to liberty of emigration and immigration; declaration of the right of the Jewish Nation to establish a national home in Palestine.[43]

The resolution was passed with an amendment that 'the opinion of the population of Palestine be ascertained'.

Ellen's anti-imperialist credentials were further demonstrated in the matter of Irish independence. At the 1918 conference of Labour women, she moved a resolution that 'this conference views with deep shame the continuance of anarchical methods of government in Ireland'. At the time, Ireland was governed by Britain, which used a paramilitary force, the notorious Black and Tans, to suppress opposition to its rule. 'Future historians', she commented

> will find it difficult to understand the incredible apathy of British people with regard to what is going on only seven hours' distance … More and more women are being arrested …conveyed to men's barracks and were often kept five or six weeks without trial … But we have got to recognize the wider significance of what is happening in Ireland. The name of Britain has become odious over the whole world.[44]

In October 1920, Ellen joined nine other representatives from the Manchester WILPF to investigate the horrors perpetrated by the Black and Tan regime in Ireland. Their conclusions were unequivocal: British troops should withdraw, political prisoners should be released and Irish people should determine their own form of government. When she returned, Ellen and the WILPF arranged a series of meetings in practically all the big cities in the United Kingdom where they spoke about the need for Irish independence. In March 1921 she was invited to give evidence to the American Commission on Ireland.[45] Her evidence was an impassioned attack on the Black and Tans, whom she accused of burning down Irish property and of intimidating the population. 'After curfew', she stated

> when the streets are in pitch darkness and no civilian may be abroad without a permit, the military lorries, armoured cars, and even tanks rattle through the streets carrying armed search parties. They batter at doors, and if the inhabitants take so much time as is needed to slip on shoes and a coat, the front door is smashed in and the house filled with armed men. They … search with the utmost brutality, tearing up mattresses, breaking open locks.[46]

In December 1921, the British government conceded. A year later Ireland was partitioned into the Irish Free State and the six counties of Ulster. Ellen complained that it was taking a long time for Ireland to be completely free of English domination.

Ellen criticised British imperialist policy in Iraq too. After the First World War Iraq was a British mandate; many Iraqis feared that this was a first step towards their country becoming part of the British Empire and rebelled. Mass demonstrations of Shia and Sunni Muslims demanded independence from British rule and the creation of an Arab government. Soon the rebellion gained momentum and armed troops challenged the British army; Winston Churchill sent in aircraft to crush the revolt and to ensure the continuation of British rule. Six thousand Iraqis and 500 British and Indian soldiers died in the conflict and costs were escalating. In Ellen's opinion, there was no doubt why Britain was involved:

> A slimy thing, oil, which is leaving traces of itself in the House of Commons ... Britain seems to be treading along the path that all great Empires have trod, to their doom. ... The Tory Imperialists are pouring out millions that are desperately needed at home for education, for housing, for employment, in order that the interests of the oil gang may be served ... these new lands have to be held down against the wishes of the vast majority of the inhabitants, and may involve us in war with the whole Mohammedan world ... but the scandal is that this Government may involve us so deeply as to make getting out of Iraq then almost as dangerous as staying in.[47]

The government took no notice of this kind of criticism and installed the British sympathiser Faysal ibn Husayn as King of Iraq to keep order among the various factions.

Throughout this period, the British government, fearful that a revolution might happen in the United Kingdom, kept a close eye on Miss Wilkinson and her comrades.[48] The government was particularly concerned about communist infiltration of the Labour Party and the unions. The Directorate of British Intelligence was convinced that Moscow, and Zinoviev in particular, were secretly helping communists to prepare a campaign to destabilise the government.

The Red International, which Ellen helped found, was considered a particular threat as it was thought better organised than any other British revolutionary group.[49] The members of the Red International were small in number but many of them were influential trade unionists who aimed to persuade their respective unions to commit to communism. Indeed, Ellen wrote a series of articles in support of communism and at the 1922 NUDAW conference proposed that it should affiliate with the Communist Party in order to break capitalism. 'It is very important', she insisted, that 'a great Trade Union like ours should make a firm stand and declare its solidarity with the left wing movement'.[50] She lost the resolution: 54,895 voted against; 17,093 voted for it.[51] In the end, the government had no need to worry as by 1922 the Communist Party was approaching bankruptcy.

Parliamentary Politics and the Labour Party

Ellen was slowly becoming aware that Parliament might be the institution through which to advance her socialist cause. She was convinced that women should be MPs, as the male House of Commons constantly interfered with the working woman, 'inspecting her, regulating her, drilling her children, bullying and arresting them, operating on them, doing everything and anything for them except feeding and clothing them'.[52] In June 1918 Ellen's chance seemed to come when she was nominated by the Lincoln and Longsight branches to be funded as a Parliamentary candidate but at the last moment she withdrew her nomination when she realised that other people had more votes than her. Nevertheless, this marked a step in her progress to the House of Commons. At the 1923 NUDAW conference it was decided to finance a further four MPs and elections took place to select them. Twenty-three candidates put themselves forward for consideration: Ellen Wilkinson came top of the poll in the ballot for Parliamentary candidates.[53] In her campaign she had argued that whereas the old trade union leaders merely wanted to make life a little easier for the workers she, as a member of the Red International, was out to break the capitalist system.[54] Her union had earlier voted decisively against affiliation to the Communist Party so it was perhaps a mark of Ellen's popularity that delegates wanted this red-headed firebrand to represent them in Parliament.

Ellen's union made it possible for her to become an MP. At the time, the majority of Labour MPs were nominees of trade unions which paid for their constituency organisation, election expenses and subsidised their salaries. In 1923, now aged 32, Ellen had a second chance and put herself forward for selection by the Gorton Labour Party. She failed to be selected, in spite of the fact that 'every wile had been used, every wire pulled on her behalf and threats and promises been implied on every side'.[55]

Meanwhile, in November 1923 Ellen gained a seat on Manchester City Council; she was the youngest council member and remained in post until 1926. However, she wanted more and tried very hard to persuade the Ashton-under-Lyne Labour Party to select her as a candidate for election. Ellen confided to her union colleague, Wright Robinson, that 'she would get Ashton if she lost Gorton' because she could buy it and 'money talked in the Labour Party'.[56] She went on to say that the other candidate who wanted Ashton 'was more popular than she was but he had no money, and although Ashton did not want her, money would speak louder than his virtues'. NUDAW expenses would cover Ellen's election expenses whereas her rival would need to rely on the impoverished local party to finance his campaign. And so Ellen Wilkinson was duly selected as the official Labour Party and union-sponsored candidate. She was already a big figure in the national trade union movement and a well-known figure in Manchester, 'widely known as a lady of considerable intellectual attainments, a capable speaker and a clever trade union and political organiser'.[57] Her election addresses were popular: the halls were packed full of supporters and those intrigued by a woman standing for election in a heavy manufacturing town. Miss Wilkinson did not disappoint. When it was impossible for audiences at the back of halls to see her, she stood on the table so that they could. In her first election speech, she criticised rich industrialists who made vast war-time profits, but who would not contribute to pay off the national debt, expecting the working class to do so instead.

At the time, Ellen was still a Communist Party member. In reply to her critics, she insisted that 'there is nothing in the Labour

Party constitution which renders her, as a Communist, ineligible as an official Parliamentary candidate'.[58] In an election speech she confirmed 'Yes, I am a Communist', defended the regime in Russia and stated 'we shall have only one class in this country, the working-class. So far as the other classes are concerned they shall be given the opportunity to work just like everyone else'.[59] Ellen nevertheless insisted that she stood as a Labour candidate, not a Communist one. Her election leaflets focused on unemployment, education, housing, government war debts, old age pensions and help for widows, rather than on communism or revolution. From now on, balancing the tensions between these two ultimately incompatible political paths would dominate her life until the outbreak of war in 1939.

A number of communists and fellow union members helped Ellen's election campaign. Wright Robinson, remarked that 'a more disreputable gang it would be impossible to find in any serious political contest. They were like a gang of freebooters out to rifle the people of Ashton out of their votes.' Ellen lost, coming third. She identified three reasons for her defeat: firstly she claimed that NUDAW had only started canvassing a fortnight before the poll so there had been little chance to gain support, secondly the Liberal candidate as ex-mayor, was a very strong opponent, thirdly Tory wealth and Tory beer had played a part. Another friend, Stella Davies, thought it was because she was too far to the left to be acceptable.[60] And as Ellen later admitted, the Ashton Labour Party did not want her.

Ellen's membership of the Communist Party was not to last. The Labour Party had deliberately adopted the method of constitutional reform and rejected the tactics of revolution. It believed in the parliamentary, not the revolutionary, road to socialism. In 1924, when the Labour Party stated that 'no member of the Communist Party shall be eligible for endorsement as a Labour Candidate' and made the Communist Party a proscribed organisation, Ellen had only two choices: either leave the Communist Party or leave the Labour Party. In March 1924 she wrote to Rajani Palme Dutt, now a communist organiser in Manchester, insisting that she would resign not on 'questions of principle but because of very strong disagreement with the policy of the Executive of the British section'. She later wrote that

'It is a bitter thing to have to do … I do not hope for mercy. Goodbye. Ellen Wilkinson'.

Her resignation from the Communist Party was announced in September 1924. Some accused Ellen of placing her career before her convictions but she denied that her departure was due to Labour Party diktats. She resigned, Ellen protested, firstly because she disliked the Communist Party's constant and indiscriminate attacks on the Labour Party; secondly she disapproved of its rejection of Parliamentary methods; thirdly she condemned its attempt to capture the trade union movement and remodel it along Russian lines; and finally she rejected its exclusive and dictatorial methods. Moreover, in her view 'the whole C.P. faction in this country seems to be increasingly unreal and out of touch with the real facts'.[61]

Ellen may have formally resigned from the Communist Party but she remained sympathetic and friendly with Dutt, signing her letters 'Nell'. She tried to get communists elected on to the Executive of her union and constantly set up or joined communist-front organisations. In June 1924, months after she had officially left, Ellen was asked to bring the Clydeside leader, James Maxton, down to a secret meeting with communists in London to discuss how factions could work together to 'establish a clear platform of issues'. At the time, she was suffering from asthma and Rajani Dutt wanted to use her well-known condition to gain sympathy. He wrote to Ellen saying that her 'illness should help to provide a sacred truce atmosphere. (Communists exploit everything) I believe you can help very much in all this if you wish. You are outside the Party (for which we shall have to attack you) but you can do big work if you get to work on this Left Wing for a definite Communist purpose.'[62] In 1927, she was still writing to 'Comrade Dutt' offering to help find finance for his beleaguered *Labour Monthly*.

Ellen may have been a revolutionary communist but at heart she embraced any organisation which promoted women's equality regardless of its political affiliations. In 1921 she became a member of the Six Point Group, a group founded by Lady Rhondda to press for changes in the law. In 1918, women over the age of 30 gained the vote but the Six Point Group wanted the vote on the same terms as men; that is, over the age of 21. On 22 February 1923, Ellen Wilkinson joined Nancy Astor, Millicent Fawcett and Eleanor Rathbone on the platform at a women's meeting in Central Hall, Westminster. It was agreed that the group would campaign for votes for women over 21, equal pay, equal moral standards, equality in industry and the professions for women.[63]

Ellen, however, remained a class-conscious feminist. In an article in *All Power*, a communist paper, she contrasted the post-war experiences of middle-class and working-class women. 'They have got votes, they can take degrees at Oxford, and they can be lawyers and chartered accountants. Which is all very useful, no doubt, but we can hardly expect Mary, who used to be an oxy-acetylene welder, and has been on the dole these two years, or Polly, skilled on the capstan lathe and now forced into domestic service, to get very excited about it.'[64]

Fortunately, Ellen did not have to wait long for another chance to be elected. Ramsay MacDonald, leader of the minority Labour government, dissolved Parliament and announced another general election for 29 October 1924. It was the third general election in three years. By now the Labour Party forbade communists to stand as Labour candidates so Ellen stood as Labour only, this time for Middlesborough East, an iron, steel and ship-building town situated on the River Tees in northeast England.

It was a hard-fought contest, especially challenging when four days before the election the British press published a letter from Grigory Zinoviev, now one of the most powerful figures in the Soviet Union, calling for increased communist agitation in England. Later, the letter was acknowledged as a forgery but by that time Labour had already been defeated. Ellen Wilkinson, however, won her seat.

3

On the Opposition Benches, 1924–29

In 1924, only 33 years old, Ellen Wilkinson took her seat in Parliament as Labour MP for Middlesborough East. She was the only woman on the opposition benches and one of only four women in the grey, masculine House of Commons. In the early days she was intensely lonely: there was no other woman to talk to on her side of the House and none of her younger men friends were there. For a time, she said, it was as if she was dropped like a stone into a quiet pond. As a stylishly dressed woman, with her bright red hair and diminutive stature, Ellen appeared a completely different kind of MP. At first she had to sit with her feet dangling six inches from the floor because of the height of the Benches in the House of Commons; 'a position of extreme discomfort', she told one reporter. She solved this by using her bulky dispatch case, full of letters from her constituents and other paperwork, as a footstool.

Ellen was delighted with her narrow victory – she won the election by a mere 927 votes. She now 'represented the heftiest men in England'.[1] Her success drew a mixed response. Some welcomed the novelty of a young woman in the House of Commons. The Women's Freedom League, which had helped in her election campaign, was jubilant because Ellen was 'a vigorous and uncompromising feminist, an exceedingly acute, tenacious, lovable and hard-headed politician'. Her union journal reported: 'Miss Wilkinson has pluck, she has charm and she has wit – a welcome change after the stodginess of the Labour intellectuals – she has more personality in her little finger than most of the Trade Union heavy fathers can boast in their whole bodies.' The *Morning Post* thought it was a pleasure to listen to her 'pleasant voice and unaffected but eminently practical utterances

Figure 3.1 Ellen's election leaflet. (USDAW)

[which] contrast sharply with the disconnected ramblings of some of her comrades.'

Others were more muted in their praise. *Labour Woman*, which one might expect to give a rousing tribute and widespread coverage of their only female MP, was still in a state of shock at losing so many able women and said little about her victory. Still others were more critical. The *Yorkshire Observer* commented that Miss Wilkinson's manner was 'decidedly and provocatively pugnacious'. The uniqueness of her position resulted in a lot of media coverage but as she commented in *The New Dawn*, 'for the Labour Party to have only one woman in Parliament is not something to be interested in, but something to be ashamed of'.

On 10 December 1924, on the second day of the Parliamentary session, Ellen Wilkinson made her first speech. It was unusual for MPs to make their maiden speeches so soon after their election. 'A really wise member of Parliament', she acknowledged, 'always waited seven years ... I didn't think that Middlesborough had sent me to the House of Commons to wait seven years ... I couldn't wait any longer because I was so indignant' about a number of injustices. The frisson of a young, attractive female MP addressing the House for the first time was too exciting for most of the male MPs to miss so a considerable number packed into the House of Commons. The only other female present was the Conservative MP, Mrs Mabel Philipson. Later Ellen confessed that she feared, as the only female Labour MP, she might become 'a sort of pet lamb ... I wanted to get into the rough and tumble of the debate ... I do not want to be regarded merely as a sort of specialist on women's issues'.

It was customary for maiden speeches to be inoffensive, innocuous and devoid of political content but Ellen had little time for this type of convention. In her maiden speech this less-than-demure red-head displayed complete self-possession and an assured speaking style. In one great sweep of a speech she put forward the need for votes for women, increased unemployment benefits, better insurance and factory law reform. The House of Commons, very predominantly male and very predominantly Conservative, gave her a 'generous cheer'. The press generally thought her 'well informed ... she is one of what we call the common people. She has lived among them and the whole dynamic urge of her actions is a burning passionate desire to better their lot'.

Ellen's combative personality had found its natural home in the belligerent and challenging atmosphere of the House of Commons. Historians often comment on the problems facing women in Parliament, pointing out how tough and unwelcoming the place could be. Ellen's suffrage days, when she had faced hostile crowds, been pelted with rotten fruit and forced to furnish witty replies to hecklers, prepared her well for the rumbustious testosterone-charged male-dominated Parliament she was later to inhabit. She may have been in a minority of four in the House of Commons but her character had been forged in rough-and-tumble politics elsewhere. Ellen's early political apprenticeship ensured that she was not afraid. She said later that there was one absolutely necessary precaution for any woman who wanted to enjoy public work and that was to grow a spiritual hide as thick as the elephant's physical one. What is certain is that Ellen had to learn to be resilient in order to balance the sometimes competing demands of her constituents, her union, her political colleagues and the socialists and feminists who saw her as their representative in Parliament.

The MP for Middlesborough startled the House of Commons in other ways. Ellen was no wallflower demurely hiding from the glances of sexually alert male colleagues. Nancy Astor and the other two women MPs always dressed soberly in black suits and white blouses, or, as one newspaper remarked, 'Quaker' attire, in order not to attract too much attention. Being a woman, they believed, was quite enough to draw comment. Ellen patently did not agree. After the Christmas recess, and only established in Parliament for a few months, she broke the sober dress conventions established by the other female members of Parliament. In February 1925 she startled the House into 'murmurs of admiration' when she wore a vivid green dress. Ellen was annoyed whenever newspapers focused on what she was wearing rather than what she thought but the press took no notice and continued to comment whenever she bought a new frock or changed her hair-style. Nancy Astor, clearly worried that Ellen's dress detracted from what she said, took her aside, talked to her in 'a motherly fashion and begged her to dress "dull". You are not here to excite an assembly already superheated on every occasion'.[2] Ellen took notice of Astor's words and reverted to the dull black and white dress adopted by other women MPs much, according to the *Empire News*, to the 'great disappointment of about 600 honourable members'.

Ellen was certainly audacious. The three other female MPs, either because they feared giving offence or were intimidated, did not use the bars, the smoking rooms or the members' cloakroom. In contrast, Ellen confronted the exclusively masculine culture. She noted that 'the Members' Cloakroom is one of those quiet places for intimate gossip in the House of Commons where a whispered word may sometimes have more effect than an hour's speech in the debating chamber', and openly criticised the lack of facilities for women in the House of Commons. At the time, women MPs squashed into a small dressing room which contained a washstand, a tin basin, a jug of cold water and a bucket – a situation that Ellen found intolerable. 'When I got into Parliament', she complained many years later, 'there were four of us to share the room that had been set apart for Lady Astor's own use when she was the only woman there, then came 8 women, then 10, but still only that same little cubby hole, with one tiny glass pane for ventilation and NO MIRROR!'[3] She also protested against certain women being excluded from the Strangers' Dining Room. For four years she worked steadily to redress these inequalities and towards the end of 1928 persuaded the Speaker to allow women to eat dinner

– but not lunch – there. Ellen capped her victory by entertaining a party of women to a celebratory vegetarian and alcohol-free meal.[4]

Ellen's first year as an MP was hectic. There was no official job description and therefore no limits placed on the amount of work she could take on. The Labour MPs' day, she said, started 'at 10am with party meetings, following on to Committees, getting through masses of correspondence when and where they could, interviewing delegations and constituents and in some cases dashing off to address large demonstrations'.[5] In her constituency, Ellen was expected to hold weekly surgeries, speak at local party meetings, visit local schools, factories and businesses, attend local functions and other events, promote the interests of her constituency in Parliament and be part-time social worker and charity distributor. In her first few weeks she tried 'to cope with my 1,394 letters and telegrams' from people who wanted advice of some sort. As the only Labour woman in Parliament, she had an 'abnormal correspondence' as lots of women turned to her for help. People expected female MPs like Ellen to be experts on all social and humanitarian questions: foreign women politicians and social workers wrote to them for information, female societies asked them to speak or take action, and many individual women wrote for help. In the House of Commons, they all felt obliged to speak in debates that concerned women leading Ellen to remark, 'as I am the only woman Member of my party in the House, I must say something'.

Ellen spoke regularly in the House of Commons, sat on Select Committees and presented Bills in Parliament. The union journal, *The New Dawn*, commented that

> behind two dancing eyes lies a brain with the quality of a filing cabinet, stored with precise and authentic details accurately card-indexed, concerning everything that affects woman, at home, at work, at play. Foodstuffs and wares, fabrics and babies, factories and pensions she has at her finger tips ... out comes file 57, section 3B, heading C, c.1. and there you are – the crushing rejoinder that destroys.[6]

Her attention to detail was a huge asset in promoting Bills in Parliament but her workload was a recipe for ill-health. In June 1926, for example, she travelled 2000 miles and spoke at 41 mass meetings. By January 1929 she was, as she wrote to Nancy Astor, 'very near the end of my strength when I spoke in the House.'[7] She had contracted a throat infection which, in the days before penicillin, was hard to cure. Chest and throat infections, exacerbated by smoking and exhaustion brought on by hard work, plagued Ellen for life.

Feminism and Socialism

Ellen Wilkinson and Nancy Astor became friends and together they made a formidable team. What is striking is the way in which the two, and indeed women MPs in general, worked closely with feminist groups outside Parliament and became willing to be the Parliamentary spokeswomen for feminist reform. Both Wilkinson and Astor cared passionately about the rights of women and established links that cut across party lines. They were said to share two traits, 'a booming voice and the ability to annoy the male members of the Commons'. Certainly the two women continually protested against the unfair legal treatment of women, a double-act which regularly exasperated male MPs on both sides of the House. Wilkinson's commitment to women's rights also made her an uncomfortable colleague particularly when she sided with the right-wing Astor against her own party and prioritised gender over class issues.

Ellen, a former suffragist activist, was implacably committed to extending the franchise to women on equal terms as men, that is over the age of 21. She worked closely with Nancy Astor, the Women's Freedom League and the National Union of Societies for Equal Citizenship (NUSEC) to secure an extension of the vote. On 20 February 1925, when she had only been an MP a few months, Ellen seconded a private members' Bill to give women suffrage equality. She prepared thoroughly for the Bills' introduction, raising the topic in the Labour Party, leading a deputation to the Home Secretary, speaking at several venues and taking part in a demonstration organised by NUSEC. The Bill, opposed by the government, failed. Nevertheless, Ellen and Nancy, acting in unison, embarrassed the

Home Secretary into confirming that Baldwin's electoral pledge of equal suffrage would be honoured.

Activists like Ellen knew that it was important to keep up public pressure if they wanted reform. In January 1926, at a meeting convened by the Women's Freedom League, she spoke in support of women's suffrage and promised the audience to keep on asking the Prime Minister when he would give votes to women over 21. This she did, asking at Prime Minister's question time on 10 February 1926 when the government intended to introduce a Bill giving equal franchise. And she asked it again in November,[8] and again in December.[9] Ellen became part of a vast new campaign launched at Central Hall, Westminster to secure votes for women over the age of 21. In June she attended an International Suffrage conference in Paris, broadcast a speech from the Eiffel Tower, and spoke at a meeting of the Actresses Franchise League in London. In July she travelled all night to walk in a suffrage procession of 3,500 women from 40 societies which included Emmeline Pankhurst, Millicent Fawcett and Charlotte Despard, but no other woman MP. Eventually, on 13 April 1927, somewhat unexpectedly, Baldwin announced that the government would give votes to women on equal terms to men.

Even so, Ellen kept prodding. Her Parliamentary colleague Nancy Astor, who believed Baldwin's promise, thought it better to cease campaigning.[10] Ellen, perhaps more politically astute or perhaps just more distrustful, did not agree. She reminded Baldwin on 21 July 1927, 'whether he is aware of the uneasiness which is being felt by many women that he does not propose to introduce equal franchise this autumn'. Eventually, on 12 March 1928, William Wedgwood Benn, on behalf of the government, introduced the Representation of the People (Equal Franchise Bill) to give women the vote on the same terms as men. There was little opposition to it in the House of Commons but it did not pass without comment from the more die-hard Conservatives. Ellen contributed to the debate, challenging those opposed to an extension of women's franchise. And when an old guard Tory expressed fears that an increase in women voters might lead to a female Chancellor of the Exchequer, she shouted out '*Why not?*' And so on 29 March 1928 'Red Ellen' witnessed one of feminism's great Parliamentary achievements when the Bill (to enfranchise women on the same terms as men) was eventually passed by 387 votes to 10. Her growing belief that the slow process of Parliamentary reform only happened with united, continuous and persistent campaigning was confirmed.

In November 1925, backed by Nancy Astor, Ellen introduced her first Bill: to permit more women to join the police forces. It might seem surprising that a left-winger like Ellen supported the extension of a police force but there were solid feminist reasons for her doing so – for example, the presence of women police officers was thought to make parks and public places safe for children. Introducing the Bill was something of an ordeal for her as she had to stand at the Bar and wait to be called by the Speaker. It seemed simple enough but at the time some 400 male MPs were watching her every move. The Bill was not opposed by the government, the Home Secretary voiced his approval and the Bill was set to be presented the next Session. On 22 June 1926, Wilkinson and Astor sponsored a Public Places (Order) Bill which advocated equal treatment of the sexes in prostitution laws and the elimination of the term 'common' prostitute from the legal code. They also put forward a Bill which legitimated children born out of wedlock whose parents subsequently married. More women police were appointed and children were legitimated but equal treatment of the sexes in prostitution had to wait until the Policing and Crime Act 2009.

Ellen and Nancy Astor, representing the women's movement, campaigned for pensions for widows with young children because they wanted to enable a widow 'to bring up her children properly at home instead of their running about the streets while she tried to scratch a living for them.'[11] However, when the Widows' Orphans and Old Age Contributory Pensions Act 1925 (which paid pensions to those over 65 and introduced widows' benefits) was introduced, Ellen objected to some of its clauses.[12] In her opinion, the Bill was full of anomalies. For example, the government wanted widows to have a flat rate of 10 shillings a week, irrespective of status, but Ellen pointed out that different rates should apply to single widows able to work and widows with children. 'Miss Wilkinson,' it was reported, 'in a very able but moderate speech, pointed out the obvious difficulties and injustices involved in this proposal. The House rose almost like one man to support her.' The Minister yielded; Miss Wilkinson won. According to the *Yorkshire Post*, Ellen was most effective in her advocacy of the cause of women during the Pensions Act. 'She carried out that fight, which had no spectacular glory attached to it, with a persistence and a logic which were altogether praiseworthy ... She was able to conduct that fight because she possesses certain qualities in a notable degree, not the showy qualities of the emotional propagandist but the sober qualities of the skilled dealer with facts.' Ellen built up each of her cases and buttressed them with hard evidence. She had, reported the paper, a House of Commons sense and never forgot that it was a legislative assembly and not a public meeting. Ellen Wilkinson and Nancy Astor harassed the Tories from their respective back-benches in other ways: in November 1925, they criticised the tax on artificial silk and in March 1926 the two protested about the decrease in funding for women's training centres.[13]

In March 1929, again supported by Nancy Astor, but also by the newly re-elected Labour women MPs, Ellen put forward a motion to introduce an Aliens Bill to amend the nationality laws.[14] The women were acting as a Parliamentary mouthpiece for the various feminist groups who were trying to change the 1914 British Nationality Act. As the law stood, a foreign woman automatically acquired British nationality on marrying a British subject whereas a British woman lost hers when she married a foreigner. The Bill provided the right for women to retain their British nationality on marriage with 'an alien' and took away the right of 'alien' women to gain British nationality on marriage. Ellen wrote to Nancy Astor asking her to back the Bill when she introduced it in Parliament.[15] When this Bill failed, Ellen and most of the other women MPs continued to press for change. On 28 November 1930, during a Second Reading of another Nationality of Women Bill, Ellen and Nancy reiterated their belief in the need for women to retain their own national identity. In the debate, Nancy praised Ellen's speech declaring, 'I only want to say "ditto" to every word she said.'[16] Their campaign eventually succeeded in 1933 when the British Nationality and Status of Aliens was passed.

In matters of equality legislation, Ellen and the other women MPs tended to vote together but in terms of economic legislation there were major differences. Ellen was a socialist feminist who believed that class parity was as important as gender equality and she was never going to be seduced by the irrepressible charm of Nancy Astor into abandoning her left-wing principles. In a speech on an Unemployment Insurance Bill, which was designed to reduce benefits, she unsheathed her socialist rapier and ripped into Nancy Astor and the Conservatives saying that they were the 'enemies of her kind of society ... their class ... has used its principles and its wealth and its privileges in order to join in the hue and cry against those who are out of work through no fault of their own but largely through the financial policy of the Government, which has enriched their class.'[17] Surprisingly, such comments did not undermine the friendship of the two MPs who continued to work together when the interests of women were paramount.

Ellen joined with union-sponsored MPs when union interests were threatened. For example, when the Conservative government wanted to deregulate the hours worked by shop workers and allow a longer working day, Ellen spoke against this. In her view, it was necessary to 'protect a section of the community who cannot protect themselves' and drew attention to the fact that the cooperative movement with which she was 'intimately associated' had decent conditions of labour, a reasonable minimum wage and a 48-hour week. She asked that the House throw out the 'carelessly drawn' Shop Bill, but her pleas were ignored and it became law.

In 1919, a Women's Department, which held annual conferences and published its own journal *Labour Woman*, was set up in the Labour Party. Ellen, who was on the Executive, was certainly a socialist and a feminist but she was different in kind from some members of the women's department. For most of her early parliamentary life, Ellen was a tear-jerking socialist rather than a brooding and agonising intellectual, a clear-headed pragmatist who wanted results rather than a purist ideologue. Soon she found herself in conflict with Labour Women activists over a number of contentious issues.

Some historians allege that, as Ellen became more well-known, she sacrificed her feminism to power and socialism. In particular, it is suggested, she compromised on birth control. At the time, it was not only illegal to sell contraceptive devices but unlawful to give out advice. In July 1924, when she was chairing the Labour Women's conference, a delegate wanted the party to campaign to make it legal for doctors to give information on birth control to married people. This generated much debate, not all of it positive, and Ellen had to chair the meeting through a very stormy and acrimonious discussion. At one point, she reproached Miss Quinn, the militantly Catholic former suffragette and trade union organiser, for using intemperate language. Quinn, who represented thousands of working women in the clothing trade, insisted that 'working mothers did not want instructions in impure and unchaste matters. Birth control was a device against God and humanity. They were not going to allow this filth'.[18] There was disorder in the conference. Ellen as Chair intervened, brought order to the meeting, insisted that she had given Miss Quinn full opportunity to express her views and would not allow her to insult other delegates. The motion in support of birth control was carried by a large majority; only six voted against. Ellen had proved to be a very effective Chair.

Publicly, Ellen equivocated over birth control. She said nothing when the Labour Party conference rejected Labour Women's proposal on the distribution of birth control information, claiming that it was an 'essentially individual and domestic matter on which it would be highly inappropriate for any political Party to dogmatise'.[19] Yet in 1926, she was the only female MP to vote for a private members' bill to allow local authorities to 'incur expenditure in conveying knowledge of birth control methods to married women who desire it'.[20] Certainly, Ellen became less vocal in her public advocacy and in 1928 even defended Arthur Henderson when he urged delegates at the Labour Women's conference not to raise the question of birth control again. She explained, somewhat disingenuously, that birth control was not a Party issue because it was not a class issue.

Her reluctance to promote birth control publicly was complicated. At the time it was a tricky issue for women's organisations as well as for ordinary people. Ellen, who was usually not frightened to speak up against injustice even when it threatened her political career, was cautious about taking sides on such a divisive issue for a number of reasons. As a single woman believed to be sexually active, she could not afford to risk any scandal or hint of notoriety. As she confided to the leading birth-control campaigner, Dora Russell, she had to be careful in her pronouncements in case she was accused of immorality.[21] Moreover, birth control was associated with the eugenic movement with its beliefs in racial supremacy and purity. A number of eugenicists correlated intelligence with social class and urged that the working class should stop producing too many children because they diluted the national stock: ideas which were anathema to Ellen. She may also have shared the socialist belief that once socialism was established there would be enough resources to feed, clothe and house all families. Even to discuss birth control meant a lack of faith in socialism's inevitable future success. In addition, Ellen may have believed that Labour Women was an ineffective tool for promoting change. It had no real voice, could not put resolutions on to the agenda of the Labour Party, and many did not take it seriously. Nearly every year Labour Women would put forward a motion at party conference, a debate would take place and, predictably, the motion would be defeated. It must also be remembered that Ellen's Middlesborough constituency was largely Catholic and she feared that any support for birth control would lose her too many precious votes.

Nevertheless, in private and behind the political scene, Ellen worked to obtain birth control reform. By this time, she realised that reform could not be achieved through conference motions or party policy and she had come to appreciate that a quieter method of campaign was necessary. Consequently, although birth control disappeared from her public statements she continued to adopt a pro-birth control stance privately and often provided Dora Russell with inside information on what she was doing unofficially. 'I have been working very hard on the birth control, and confidentially', she declared, 'I find ... the position is now that the local authorities can do as they please in this matter. What I want is to get an official statement from the Minister in Parliament, but he is taking his time. However, I am hoping to get it through.'[22] Eventually, in July 1930, Arthur Greenwood, Minister for Health in the Labour government, presented Memorandum 153 to the Cabinet and it was passed. The Memorandum permitted local authorities, if they wished, to provide birth control clinics and information to married mothers about birth control 'where further pregnancy would be detrimental to health'. Privately, and without generating too much fuss, Ellen had achieved the result for which Labour Women had so publicly and acrimoniously campaigned.

There were further tensions between Ellen and other Labour Party feminists. A number of feminists, including Ellen, suggested that married women be given a family allowance by the state if they cared for their children at home. In this way, they argued, women's unpaid work in the home was rewarded and married women given some measure of financial independence. Not everyone agreed. Some feminists believed that family allowances consolidated women's role in the home and thus diverted them from the struggle for equal pay. Ellen, conscious of the poverty of working-class families, especially in times of strikes and industrial distress, thought otherwise. She lost this battle: both the TUC and NUDAW rejected the idea of family allowances. Later, Ellen too changed her mind – twice: in 1938 she was against family allowances; by 1945 she supported them once more.

Protective legislation, that is laws which reduced the hours worked by women and children, was another controversial question for both feminists and socialists. Some Labour Women disliked protective laws because they feared that if women and children were treated as special cases it would damage their chances of equality. Others, like Ellen, believed that women needed all the protection they could get. In March 1926 in one of the most eloquent speeches that session, Ellen introduced her private members' Bill to the House of Commons. It was a Factory Bill which would give a 38-hour week for women and young people, safer machinery, better health, lighting, ventilation and sanitation. It was the first Factory Act since 1902 with 143 clauses and four schedules. Ellen gave a 'very effective speech' and was 'embarrassed with congratulations'. She had, thought the *Scotsman*, dropped the 'rancorous tone which distinguished her earlier speeches and the House now listens to her with rapt attention'. The Factory Bill was praised on all sides – and then defeated by the Tories. But one of Ellen's many strengths was her tenacity; if she believed in a cause, she never gave up: three years later she led a deputation to J.R. Clynes, Labour Home Secretary, to persuade him of the need to protect women workers.[23] Once again, her campaign failed.

Ellen and some leading Labour Women even disagreed about the relationship between the women's section and the Labour Party. At the 1929 Labour Women conference, Dora Russell argued that Labour Women should create party policy on women. In a veiled criticism of Wilkinson, Russell contended 'there were times when they [i.e. women on the Executive of the Labour Party] felt themselves more in the light of officials of the Party than representatives of the women'. Everyone at the conference, of course, would know to whom she referred. In defence, Wilkinson pointed out that it was neither possible nor desirable to have Labour Women responsible for creating women's policy because it would create 'a cleavage right through the movement between the men and women.'[24] In her view, party policy should be thrashed out at the Labour Party conference with everyone in the party contributing rather than at fringe meetings of the women's section.

Fighting the Tories

Before the First World War, London had been the financial capital of the world but post-war Britain was a very different country. The pound was weakened against the dollar, industrial output from coal, cotton and shipbuilding declined even further and unemployment rose. Ellen insisted that the bankers were controlling policy and that the Chancellor 'just moved up and down as a barometer or puppet of the bankers' little game'. The bankers' interests, she maintained, ran counter to the interests of those who worked. Moreover, the banks and the bankers were much more powerful than the Houses of Parliament. She believed that there was a choice between 'sham democracy controlled by international finance or real democracy controlled by the people'.

Unusually for a woman MP, Ellen often spoke in economic debates, maintaining a fierce criticism of the government's economic strategies. For example, during the third reading of a Bill to bring Britain back on the gold standard, she protested that it would damage British business, make British goods uncompetitive and lead to unemployment. 'I feel', Ellen said 'that we are paying a very high price for the smiles of the financiers of America.'[25] In her opinion the unemployed would be forced to bear the cost, declaring that it was 'easier for a camel to go through the eye of a needle than for an unemployed man to get his insurance benefit'.

On Monday, 3 May 1926, the TUC called a General Strike. Millions of workers stopped work in support of the coal miners who had had their wages reduced. 'God make us worthy of the men we lead', was Ellen's prayer. For those fateful nine days she was one of several flying squads of speakers who drove cars around the country, holding meetings in each town. She, along with Frank Horrabin, started at Oxford and wove around the Midland towns stopping at Banbury, Woodford, Coventry, Walsall, Wolverhampton, Stafford, Crew, Worcester, Hereford and Shrewsbury, before heading north to Darlington, Stockton, Middlesborough and York. Everywhere she visited the strike was solid. As all public transport was stopped, men and women walked 10 or 15 miles, often in the rain, to hear her speak. Her supporters believed that Ellen's delightfully warm personality, great charm, courage and quick wit allowed her to face even potentially hostile audiences and respond to hecklers without fear or embarrassment. Her detractors saw her as a communist in Labour clothes deliberately fomenting unrest. Nine days later, to Ellen's surprise and disgust, the TUC called off the strike and everyone, apart from the miners, returned to work. The miners, demanding 'not a penny off the pay, not a minute off the day' remained on strike for a further six months. Ellen later helped immortalise the strike in two books. Her co-authored *A Workers History of the Great Strike* is an emotionally charged account of the nine days of the strike and her autobiographical novel *Clash* captures the atmosphere, excitement and frustration of the strikers, its officials and grassroots supporters.

The Minister of Health, Neville Chamberlain, vowed that striking miners would receive 'not one scrap of assistance' and reduced outdoor relief to below unemployment benefit. In England, food coupons were given to women and children; in Scotland, women and children were fed in large centres. The men went hungry. Ellen became Chair of the Women's Committee for the Relief of Miners' Wives and Children, an organisation set up to fund-raise for miners' families most in need. As ever, she threw herself into her work, this time raising money to feed the families of miners. Ellen remarked that she could neither sleep nor eat until funds had reached such proportions that there was no starving woman or child left unprovided. 'The most vivid imagination', she maintained, 'can conjure up no scene of desolation, human suffering and hopelessness to surpass what actually met my eyes in the mining districts. Hungry women and children, stoical patient men, weary with inactivity.' She told pitiable stories of children who were too hungry to walk to school, of others whose boots were in pawn and who had to go barefoot to the soup kitchens, of babies whose features bore the mark of coming death from malnutrition, and of emaciated women who went without food so that their children could eat. By January 1927 the fund had raised £313,844; at one meeting alone Ellen raised £1,000.[26] This was nowhere near enough to feed the full contingent of striking miners and their families so she went to America to raise more money.

'Red Ellen' tried to shock people into sympathy with the miners. On 5 June 1926 she wrote a provocative column in *Lansbury's Labour Weekly* entitled 'Cheaper than Horseflesh'. In her article she alleged that 1,500 boys and men employed in the mines at Radstock, Somerset worked 'stark naked, on all fours, with a rope round their waist and a chain between their legs hitched on to a wagon' which they pulled through the mine.[27] The rope, she claimed, rubbed off the skin until callouses were formed, dirt got in and septic wounds resulted. 'The nation prosecutes if a pit pony is worked with bleeding sores,' she declared, but 'no one worries when it's only a lad. He is cheaper than horseflesh.' This inflammatory article caused uproar in the press and in Parliament. Ellen's critics denied her facts, challenged her evidence and denounced her as inflammatory and a bamboozler.

Soon after her offending article and while the miners were still on strike, the Tory government introduced a Coal Mines Bill. On 28 June 1926, during the second reading of the Coal Mines Bill, Ellen responded to her critics in her own unique way by producing a rope with a chain attachment and holding it up for MPs to see. 'This', declared Ellen

is the rope that goes round the man's waist; this is the chain that passed between his legs, and this is the crook that is hitched on to the tub ... The collieries in which these men are working are very hot. The wearing of either no clothes or the very barest minimum of clothes is an absolute necessity, because the heat is so great. There is no proper ventilation.[28]

The harness, she announced, 'was being worn by a miner not 60 years ago but on the 30th April of this year'. The Tory government responded to her melodramatic piece of theatre by reducing wages, increasing working hours and permitting working conditions to deteriorate.

In December, six months after the General Strike had ended, the hungry miners, beaten into submission, were forced to return to work on the owners' terms, which meant longer hours, lower pay and the victimisation of strikers. Ellen blamed the defeat on TUC officials and Labour Party timidity. In her first major speech to the Labour Party conference in 1926 she urged the front bench of her own party to come out tougher against the Tories: they should, Ellen asserted, hold up the government, and not make agreements with the other side. 'They should fight and fight all the time', she insisted. Many of the delegates felt her speech was too emotional but the Miners' Federation expressed its gratitude to women like Miss Wilkinson for 'having saved the British Labour Movement from disgrace'.[29]

In 1927, a newly confident Conservative government passed the Trades Disputes Act which restricted workers' rights even further. It made sympathetic strikes illegal, banned civil servants from joining unions affiliated to the TUC, protected blacklegs, and made picketing almost impossible. Ellen insisted that the object of the Bill was to break up feelings of solidarity among the workers. 'People who denounced the Conservative Party as stupid', she declared, 'make me tired. In the things they care about, the Tory leaders are clear-sighted and determined men.'[30] Ever since the Conservative government was returned to power, she claimed, they had worked steadily, and deliberately, in the interests of a very few rich people. In the view of her detractors, she was merely voicing 'a passionate and relentless class bitterness'.

This Act made it harder for unions to raise political funds for the Labour Party. Instead of members 'contracting out' of paying a levy to the Labour Party they now had to 'contract in'. This, Ellen told friends, had reduced the income of the Labour Party by 50 per cent. Her union thought that the Bill represented 'the most serious and deliberate attack upon the established rights and legal powers of trade unions that has been made during the past hundred years. It is a calculated attempt to cripple the trade unions and to destroy the political Labour party.' The Bill was considered to be 'inspired by motives of class and partisan hostility … and is designed to deprive the workers of their effective powers of resistance.'[31] Privately, Ellen was very worried about the political levy: she wrote to her old comrade Rajani Palme Dutt that it 'has done the Labour Party more harm than it cares to confess. Our Union has made superhuman efforts to get the forms in … no hostility to signing, just inertia.'[32]

In 1927, in recognition of her growing Parliamentary reputation, Ellen was elected to the National Executive of the Labour Party (NEC). She was on her way to becoming a key figure in the Labour Party and in a good position to help shape party policy. At the time, the NEC played a significant role in the Labour Party, and was responsible for designing and communicating party policy. Ellen was a member of a newly created Special Sub-Committee of the NEC whose brief included setting out the broad proposals for the next election. She was also on the Press and Publicity Department responsible for issuing party pamphlets, new publications, and leaflets. Ellen confided to Palme Dutt that 'you may have seen from the Press that I am now on the NEC. They have put me on the Programme Committee and the Living Wage Enquiry. The Programme Committee is of the first importance but it is curiously difficult to produce a programme for a Party which hasn't a philosophy.'[33] At the 1927 Labour Party conference, she appealed to delegates to make the party's programme a 'very bold programme', because the working classes wanted a bold lead 'to deal with the situation, the terrible situation of poverty and destitution in which they found themselves'. She urged that 'instead of thinking of their socialism as something to be attained thousands of years hence – to think of it as something that could be attained in their time if only they had the will, the passion, and the determination to put it through'.[34]

Ellen was a quick learner, often adapting her language and style to suit her listeners. Where she perceived it was in her best interests to adopt an uncompromising stance on one position or another, she would do so, especially if this was for the benefit of a particular audience e.g. her trade union sponsors who carried high expectations of her performance. Her success as a politician owes as much to her ability to play to the gallery as it did to her realistic outlook and her increasingly pragmatic approach to politics.

4

In and Out of Power, 1929–35

I n May 1929, Ellen Wilkinson fought her second General Election. It was an expensive time for her: money was urgently needed for publicity leaflets, speakers' expenses, the hire of halls and the salary of an election agent. In the past NUDAW had taken care of all expenses, but the union, its political funds depleted by the Trades Disputes Act 1927, could only contribute 75 per cent towards her election costs. Ellen used £100 from her recently-published novel and donations from friends to help defray election costs.[1] It was set to be a challenging contest.

As a member of the NEC's Press and Publicity Department, Ellen was responsible for writing, editing and distributing election literature: leaflets, pamphlets, posters, speakers' notes, election specials and even lantern films. She also helped write the draft programme outlining Labour policy. Most people in the NEC favoured a very long statement with vague ideals, but Ellen argued for a short statement that presented in 'unmistakable terms' concrete and lucid proposals. Her advice was ignored and the resulting manifesto, *Labour and the Nation*, was thought to be much too hazy.

Nonetheless, the election, fought against a background of rising unemployment and memories of the General Strike, returned a minority Labour government for the second time. On 4 June, Ramsay MacDonald once more became Prime Minister. By now, thanks to the efforts of Ellen and other sympathetic MPs, all women over the age of 21 were eligible to vote in what was condescendingly called the 'Flapper Election'. Fourteen women MPs were elected, nine of whom were Labour. Ellen, who increased her majority by 3,199, was delighted.

Ramsay MacDonald, perhaps mindful of the new electorate, promoted women to key posts. Two well-established Labour figures

Figure 4.1 Ellen and Labour women MPs, 1929. Back row: Marion Phillips, Edith Picton-Turbeville, Ethel Bentham and Mary Hamilton. Front row, left to right: Cynthia Mosley, Susan Lawrence, Margaret Bondfield, Ellen Wilkinson and Jenny Lee. (Hayes Peoples History)

who had served in the first Labour government were appointed: Margaret Bondfield as Minister of Labour and Susan Lawrence as Parliamentary Secretary to the Ministry of Health. At this point Ellen was promoted and given the post of Parliamentary Private Secretary to Susan Lawrence. Beatrice Webb confided to her diary that Ellen, whom she considered to be 'far more efficient and more popular than either Susan or Margaret', was 'becoming moulded for office'. Conscious of Ellen's health, Beatrice Webb believed that she had a big political career before her, 'if she does not work herself out by rattling over the country'.[2] In 1929 Ellen lost her place on the NEC but it was a measure of her growing reputation that in October that year she was appointed to serve on the Donoughmore Commission, a Royal Commission set up to investigate the powers exercised by civil servants and ministers. To serve on a Royal Commission was a defining feature of her growing prestige and a move towards becoming established as a senior Labour Party politician.

Ellen continued to work extraordinarily hard. Each day she got up at 6 a.m., wrote her articles until 9 a.m., then spent the rest of the morning dealing with one of the heaviest postbags of any MP. As well as dealing with constituency issues, her new job involved looking after Susan Lawrence, helping with her correspondence, meeting her visitors, receiving deputations, arranging visits to her by other MPs and sitting behind her boss in the House of Commons ready with information. It was known to be self-sacrificing and self-obliterating work with one saving grace – it was viewed as a ministerial apprenticeship. Ellen was 'full of admiration and affection' for her new boss, who was seen to restrain some of her wilder ideas. Rather than mull over unrealistic and unrealisable goals, Susan Lawrence prevailed on Ellen to work for the improvement of conditions for mothers and babies in hospitals and for more and better maternity clinics. She asked Ellen to help steer a Mental Health Bill through Parliament: this made it possible for people to be treated in mental institutions without having to be certified as lunatics. It received the Royal Assent on 10 July 1930.

Ellen continued to sponsor Bills which concerned NUDAW members, women and her constituency. During the second reading of the Shop (Hours of Employment) Bill, which proposed a 48-hour week for shop workers, she railed against those Conservatives who opposed it. 'The only difference', she declared, 'between the old Tory and the young Tory is that the young Tory gives sympathy, but both are equally concerned that nothing should be done'.[3] The Bill was referred to a Standing Committee for further consideration but did not become law. Her other Bill, concerning hire purchase reform, also failed at this time.

Ellen shared Arthur Greenwood's philosophy of the right of working people to decent housing: she supported his 1930 Housing Act which provided subsidies for slum clearance and for new dwellings to be built. Londoners, she commented, 'strike one as having an infinite capacity for being uncomfortable. … Their forbears must have belonged to the Antiquated Society of Sardine Packers'. When she visited some of the houses in northeast England she was confronted by rotten floors, leaky roofs, damp walls where paper hung away in loose strips and she listened to stories of babies being bitten by rats. In a newspaper article entitled 'Caravan Colony', a place immortalised in her friend Winifred Holtby's book *South Riding*, she protested about the shabby one-storey wooden buildings and old railway carriages: how every drop of water had to be carried from a tap which served seven families, how the cooking stove made the cramped living-room almost intolerable, how leaking roofs were a frequent problem in wet weather and how the land around the buildings turned into a swamp when it rained. 'I came away', she declared 'amazed at the heroism of the working-class woman in trying to make the best of the worst possible conditions'.

Economic Turmoil

On 29 October 1929 the Wall Street Crash precipitated a worldwide economic crisis. Banks collapsed, businesses went bust, consumer spending plummeted, currencies lost their status and unemployment rose. Ellen wrote to a friend saying 'it looks like being a difficult world for a bit, doesn't it?'[4]

The Labour government had an economic choice: it could either cut expenditure or spend its way out of recession. Ellen, with others on the left, believed that Britain should abandon the gold standard and devalue the pound thus reducing the price of British goods and making them easier to sell abroad. She also wanted the government to introduce a 'living wage', offer cheap credit to the working class and, influenced by Keynes, spend its way out of recession. Unfortunately, the Chancellor of the Exchequer, Philip Snowden, was an orthodox economist who believed in balanced budgets and convinced most of the Cabinet that economic retrenchment, rather than expansion, would restore confidence and prosperity to Britain. Consequently, the Labour government put up taxes and reduced government expenditure. The squeeze, the Governor of the Bank of England urged, was essential for restoring the economy to health; nationalising the Bank of England, countered Ellen, was essential for restoring the country's wealth. The government's austerity programme strategies, she argued, hit the poorer sections of society the hardest. Few attempts were made to spend money on employment generation or on investment in distressed areas in order to boost growth.

This was 1930, not 2010, yet Ellen knew exactly where to place the blame for this economic catastrophe: the greed of the bankers. In her view, the City of London had loaned money in order to reap immense, and ultimately unsustainable, profits but instead 'had been caught out with heavy losses in speculation'. 'We are told', she thundered 'that the Budget doesn't balance, that there are going to be terrible things happen unless you are prepared to accept cuts – cuts everywhere except in the dividend of the Bankers'. In her view, the world was not suffering from over-production but under-consumption and she urged that 'the sooner we ... increase the buying power of the poorer classes the sooner we will get out of this depression'.

In December 1930, the Labour government set up a Royal Commission, the Gregory Commission, to examine unemployment and the funding of it. Ellen initially welcomed the Commission since it would 'blow sky high the campaign of lies' which some papers published about the unemployed. At the time, there were scare stories about large numbers of people falsely claiming benefits, stories which she condemned. In her view, the standard of financial morality among the working class was far higher than among bankers. 'There are fewer men sent to prison for benefit fraud', she insisted, 'than there are city financiers who have enjoyed Her Majesty's hospitality'. When the Commission reported in June 1931 it recommended a 30 per cent cut in benefits.

The Labour Party rejected most of the stringent measures advocated by the Royal Commission and set up another, the May Committee, which was composed of bankers and financial experts. When it reported at the end of July 1931 it recommended that millions of savings should come from increased unemployment insurance contributions and a reduction of (only!) 20 per cent in benefits. After a number of very tense Cabinet meetings, cuts were agreed. Too late – the economy was already in free-fall and the misery of those already unemployed, underemployed and poorly paid was set to worsen.

Still enthralled by the Soviet Republic and still a Marxist at heart, Ellen echoed the current socialist belief that a planned economy was the only real solution to the economic crisis. Capitalism, she maintained, was an unworkable, wicked system. In communist Russia, she wrote, there was no unemployment as there was an 'adjustment of Labour to the different tasks required by the State'. Russia, she believed, was succeeding because the fundamental idea was right. 'We have', she argued, 'to meet this financial situation by measures to re-organise our industry and save it from the chaos to which capitalist competition and imperialist war has brought it'. She was in favour of public control of the banking system and nationalising the 'commanding heights of industry'. It is time, she insisted, for workers' control: 'time that they planned it, organised it, and developed it so that all might enjoy the wealth which we can produce'. For Ellen, nationalisation and planning were the means of introducing order and stability to a roller-coaster economy. Her critics claimed that Miss Wilkinson wanted to 'nationalise the cow'.

At the same time, Ellen tried everything to promote Middlesborough steel products. In a debate on the steel industry in November 1930 she urged the government to think imaginatively about steel and even suggested using it to build houses and design new furniture. As ever, she put her ideas into practice by equipping her flat with steel tables and chairs. In an impassioned plea to the House of Commons, Ellen urged that in view of the grave unemployment in the country, particularly in the heavy steel and iron industries the House

> should energetically explore every avenue which will lead to increased trade with the Russian Soviet Republic ... I will indicate a few of the things that are needed by Russia. Forty-two new power stations. Think what that would mean for the Metropolitan Vickers Company! New motor units for Leningrad and Nijni Novgorod. Twelve new blast furnaces for the Ukraine ... within the next three years £180,000,000 will be invested by Russia in industrial plant abroad.[5]

And, as she sardonically noted, this would create 'real beneficial employment, instead of putting men on to such jobs as titivating roads'.[6] Her appeals were ignored.

The new Labour government, which had promised to ameliorate unemployment, was demoralised. Critics saw it as incompetent and directionless. It was in a difficult position: the Conservatives were a determined opposition, the Liberals only intermittent supporters and the House of Lords was as obstructive as ever to a left-leaning Parliament. In this situation, even the critical Ellen agreed, it was well-nigh impossible to promote genuinely socialist measures or even to put into practice Labour's rather meagre plans for public works. When the government passed the Coal Mines Act 1930 which reduced working hours, and the Land Act 1931 which would have given Labour power to buy land, these were either ignored or undermined by the House of Lords. 'In a country that calls itself a democracy', she complained, 'it really is a scandal that an unelected revising chamber should be tolerated, in which the Conservative Party has a permanent and overwhelming majority'.[7]

Ellen, who never baulked at upsetting anyone if the cause was justified, joined forces with Eleanor Rathbone, Jennie Lee and Cynthia Mosley, to champion the rights of women against her own party's leadership and that of other Labour Party feminists. The economic crisis had persuaded the Minister of Labour and former trade union official, Margaret Bondfield, to pass an Anomalies Act aimed at stamping out so-called abuses of the unemployment benefit system. At 4.30 a.m. on 15 July 1931, Bondfield proposed a clause which would disqualify 180,000 married women from claiming benefits. The Labour MP and editor of *Labour Woman,* Dr Marion Phillips gave her support. Ellen vehemently disagreed with her Labour colleagues. In her view, the clause raised 'the old, bad principle of discrimination against women, which the whole women's movement has been fighting against since about 1870'.[8] Her cries remained unheeded and the Labour government passed the clause on the basis that married women were not 'genuinely seeking work'. Ellen fought other clauses that took away benefits with equal vigour.

The debate on the Anomalies Act presaged the break-up of the Labour government. It eventually collapsed on 23 August 1931 when Ramsay MacDonald forced the Cabinet to vote on the recommended cuts and only 11 out of 20 Ministers voted in favour. MacDonald resigned as Labour leader and became Prime Minister of a newly constituted National coalition government. By now, Ellen was completely disillusioned with him and his faction believing their actions to be 'the most flagrant example of treachery – that of leaders deserting their followers in a moment of crisis'.[9] She was publicly contemptuous of MacDonald, whom she felt had betrayed the party and like all the other Labour women MPs and most of the men, she refused to join the National government.

On 8 September 1931, when Parliament met after the summer recess, all those paid by the state, from cabinet ministers to the unemployed, had their pay or benefits cut by 10 per cent. The exceptions were the police who had their pay cut by 5 per cent and teachers by 15 per cent. Not surprisingly, Ellen, along with the TUC and most of the Labour Party, disagreed with the stringent measures put forward by MacDonald and the newly formed National government. Time and time again, she reiterated her belief that bankers' greed was responsible for the crisis. Ellen was furious and railed against the 'cuts in teachers' salaries, Army and Navy, police-cuts – cuts everywhere except in the dividend of the bankers'. She saw no reason why the 'meagre bread ration of the unemployed should be cut to a more miserable pittance', and argued that the crisis was an 'artificial one brought about by blundering bankers'. At the same time as reducing benefits, the government imposed the Family Means Test on all those unemployed for more than six months. By the beginning of 1932 nearly one million people were subject to its meanness.

Her good friend and fellow radical Harold Laski, another Mancunian, tells of a moment when Ellen confronted MacDonald over the operation of the means test. 'He said with measured coldness that he could not afford, over so large an issue, to be sentimental. I was proud of the way in which Ellen, tossing that red mane, and with fire blazing from her eyes, spoke her mind about the type of politician who thinks that safeguarding the poor against the abyss of destitution and unemployment was sentimentality.' Ellen had learned her Methodist texts well. Her outburst, Laski said, was like the angry diatribe of an Old Testament prophet. The Prime Minister retreated nervously and apologetically.

The last few months of 1931 flew past quickly for Ellen. On 28 September 1931 Ramsay MacDonald was expelled from the Labour Party. On the same day, Ellen Wilkinson led Middlesborough's biggest political demonstration of several thousand unemployed men and women. Speaking on a cart surrounded by mothers and young babies, she told her audience that capitalism was wicked and should be replaced by something better. On 5 October MacDonald called a General Election, to take place on 27 October. Ellen was anxious about her own prospects and that of the Labour Party's, judging that 'it seems impossible at the moment to imagine any result that will not be disastrous'.[10]

Ellen brought her 'economy' car to Middlesborough but insisted that she planned to do most of her electioneering on foot. She bought a stout pair of shoes and woollen stockings from a local shop. 'I am always interested to note how much cheaper prices are in Middlesborough' she remarked, rather insensitively, to those who were struggling to buy basic necessities. She stood against a sole Liberal candidate and confessed to being nervous about the election, commenting 'I do hope it is going to be better than it looks.' In the past, she had been scathing about the Liberal Party and its chance of electoral success, once savagely remarking that she 'could not say much about the Liberal Party, because they were taught not to speak ill of the dead'.

Election meetings were rougher than normal: at one open-air meeting, Ellen's eye was injured by a firework thrown over a wall by some young boys and the meeting was held up until a chemist could attend to her. She concluded her talk with a handkerchief wrapped round the affected eye. Another time, police had to escort her from an open-air meeting when a crowd of Liberals subjected her to hoots, cat-calls and other interruptions. Once, when Ellen was alone in a quiet street, she was attacked by a group of six or seven fur-coated women wearing Liberal colours, who broke a window of her car, tore off its party ribbons, bashed the lamp, and hammered her with the steel frames of their handbags. She was left with a bruised shoulder. Yet Ellen's supporters could be rough and disruptive too: she had to insist that her Liberal opponent be given a quiet hearing. 'Shouting', she told them 'settled nothing .... The refusal of free speech to either candidate makes the working of democracy impossible'.

The National government, led by Ramsay MacDonald, won a landslide victory securing 554 seats: all at the expense of Labour, who won a humiliating 52. It was a crushing defeat for Labour, made worse when several leading figures, including Herbert Morrison, Emanuel Shinwell, Frederick Pethick-Lawrence, Hugh Dalton, Margaret

Bondfield, Susan Lawrence and Arthur Greenwood lost their seats. Not one of the nine Labour women was re-elected.

Out of Parliament, 1931–35

When Parliament opened on 10 November 1931, Ellen Wilkinson was not there. Instead, a Liberal who won 18,409 votes to Ellen's 12,080 represented Middlesborough. The whole framework of her life suddenly crumbled. Devastated by her defeat, she spoke of how it was 'too painful to look at the Labour benches and remember the men and women who were not there'.[11] She insisted that the Labour Party was defeated not because it was socialist, 'but because it was not Socialist enough'. She blamed the Press, the BBC, the Church and the cinema for defeat, and accused Lord Beaverbrook, owner of a number of right-wing newspapers, for using scare-mongering tactics to convince voters of the dangers of a socialist government.[12] In her view, the Labour Party had lost its direction. She thought it better to have

> a small disciplined party that knows what it wants than a huge mass of people whose allegiance to Labour is little more than a vague humanitarian sentiment. If this defeat is the cause of the Labour Party facing facts, and cutting away a lot of the pretence of the last two years, the sacrifice of so many fine comrades will not have been in vain.[13]

In the early 1930s Ellen's politics became increasingly radical and her role as the party's left-wing conscience strengthened. No longer constrained by her role as an MP, she wrote uncompromisingly radical and deliberately provocative articles for the popular press. The range of her activities in this period was breath-taking, despite her recurring bronchial and lung infections. She remained committed to women's equality, fought for the rights of the working class and unemployed and devoted much of her boundless energy into a vigorous campaign against fascism.

The early years of the 1930s were challenging for Ellen. She not only lost her seat in Parliament but with it her place on the NEC, and her delegate status at the National Labour conferences. She coped with these difficulties with her usual optimism and spirited defiance, putting on a brave face and insisting that her defeat had been a steep, yet essential, learning curve. During this time, Ellen needed to earn a living so she resumed full-time work for NUDAW, she lectured and she developed her reputation as a writer. She published a number of books including *The Division Bell Mystery* (1932), a crime novel set in the House of Commons, as well as co-authoring political treatises such as *The Terror in Germany* (1933), *Why Fascism?* (1934), *Why War?* (1934) and the *Condition of India* (1934). Ellen had a natural journalistic flair and an ability to popularise difficult and contentious issues. Consequently she contributed regularly to newspapers and journals: *Clarion*, *Time and Tide*, the *Daily Herald*, *John Bull*, the *Daily Express*, the *Daily Mirror*, the *Daily Mail*, *New Leader*, *Pearson's Weekly*, the *Star* and the *Sunday Referee*.

In February 1931, Ellen was guest Parliamentary correspondent for the *Daily Express*. She spoke of how nervous she felt when she arrived at the Press Gallery; she was the first-ever female press reporter to sit in the Gallery and said she felt like an interloper. In her articles, she insisted that a powerful and challenging opposition was necessary to good governance and berated the MPs in the House of Commons for looking too much alike. 'The House', she wrote, 'is too much like a perfectly cast drawing room comedy on a West End stage'.[14] Soon she was a regular correspondent for the *Daily Express* and two of her novels, *Clash* and *The Division Bell Mystery*, were serialised in the paper. Ellen was not a high-quality novelist but the autobiographical topicality of the books made them very appealing to the readership of the *Express*.

In 1933, she was delighted to be taken on as one of *Time and Tide's* correspondents. The journal was a weekly political and literary review magazine which had begun as a forum for the Six Point Group. Vera Brittain, Winifred Holtby, Virginia Woolf, Storm Jameson, Rebecca West and D.H. Lawrence all wrote for the paper, so it was a sign of Ellen's authorial reputation that she was asked to join them. She wrote a monthly column under her own name, but also wrote under a pseudonym, 'East Wind', particularly if the topic was risqué or politically contentious. In September 1934, Winifred Holtby wrote to

Vera Brittain that '*Time and Tide* is going to publish an article about a Paris brothel (really written by Ellen Wilkinson, but that's private) very rousing ... We shall get into trouble, but good trouble, I think'.[15]

Ellen admitted that 'meeting and being accepted by the *Time and Tide* group, has been a big thing to me this last 12 months or so. Politics have become so barren somehow'.[16] She admired *Time and Tide's* founder Lady Rhondda who became a good friend. Ellen's self-confidence was not so firmly held as people assumed. In a letter to Winifred Holtby she confessed: 'I can't explain but I was horribly worried about doing "Notes" this Jan: if you knew how much your appreciation has meant. I felt when I came back from India that I simply couldn't write a line anymore.'[17] Later, she wrote that she was getting nervous about her monthly 'Notes' as 'to live up to a standard set by folk like you, Rebecca West and Rose Macaulay is rather terrifying'.[18]

It was at this time that Ellen honed her feminism and socialism and sharpened her polemic skills. Blessed with a ceaselessly energetic disposition, in spite of health problems, she was an indefatigable worker. She used her time out of office to campaign for the causes close to her; she held fervent beliefs and was not afraid to express them strongly when it involved class and gender issues. Her utterly uncompromising views on women, the working class, economics and the government must have both delighted and infuriated in equal measure. To some she was a beacon of socialist and feminist light in the Conservative darkness; to others she was egotistical, intransigent, and much too left-wing for comfort. Whatever people thought of her, one of Ellen's major, and continuing, concerns was the raft of inequalities suffered by women. In a series of deliberately provocative articles in the popular press she flaunted her radical credentials to a wide audience.

Her feminist torch remained undimmed. In newspaper articles, she protested about the prejudices held against women and argued that because men had made a mess of finance, business and government, women should be given the opportunity to improve matters. In her view, men had not only made an 'uncomfortable world', but had refused to share that world with women. 'The only women that men will accept in public life', Ellen grumbled, 'are women of whom it can be said "she has a brain like a man's"'.

In her opinion, female MPs were better than their male equivalent. Eleanor Rathbone, she argued, was 'worth 10 ordinary male MPs'. In an article for the *Daily Express* Ellen wrote that the 'time is coming when we shall have a woman as Prime Minister', since she believed that women could not possibly make a 'worse mess of it' than men. She thought that, in essence, politics was a woman's job rather than a man's because politics was only housekeeping on a larger scale. Moreover, she wrote, women did not have the 'abnormal respect' for vested interests that male politicians displayed, since no woman would stand 'flabbily around and let the experts prove that though there is plenty of everything – men, money and machines – we must all scrimp and suffer because of "economic laws"'.[19]

Ellen continually hammered away at the different means by which women were subjugated by marriage. In one article for *Pearson's Weekly*, entitled 'Marriage as a Dangerous Trade', she maintained that the root of the problem 'is that people will only think of a woman, not as an individual, but as linked up with someone else'. In her opinion marriage was hazardous for women. More women, she maintained, died from childbirth than from workplace accidents. The death and sickness rate among married women, especially mothers, 'is so high as to make marriage a much more dangerous occupation than minding a machine in a factory. For every class of woman worker the law lays down regulations for air space, ventilation, lighting and heating, weekend rest, hours of work, but the married woman enjoys no such protection.' She felt it outrageous that the law regarded a man's wife as his property to do with pretty much as he liked, with the result was that husbands were let off with a trivial fine for 'brutal ill treatment' of their wives.

The conventional view that married women should stay at home if their husbands earned enough to keep them was hateful to Ellen. Those who dared to marry, she complained, were unfairly dismissed from their jobs before the 'wedding certificate was dry'. Ellen was equally aghast that women lost their economic dignity on marriage, had their personal incomes added to that of their husbands for tax purposes, found it difficult to gain credit and almost impossible to do business. To add insult to injury, women still lost their nationality when they married a foreigner.

To sympathetic audiences, 'Red Ellen' was unambiguously left-wing. At the 1932 Labour Women conference, she spoke on a report on 'How Women Fare under Reactionary Government', urging conference that

> if they want a decent life for the people, a chance for the children … they had to get rid of the capitalist system … . They now had to face the end of a period of benevolent democratic capitalism which was prepared to give concessions in order to keep its profits – that had now gone, and in all naked ugliness the real class war was there. If they wanted a decent life they had got to have national reorganization, national ownership and control of the means of life.[20]

Yet there were times at the conference when other feminists, usually those from more middle-class backgrounds, found her beliefs objectionable. Ellen, who wanted a shorter day and better working conditions for working-class women, exasperated delegates who believed that women should be treated the same as men. Relations between the two were strained further when she made inflammatory comments such as 'it was no use the type of woman who had never seen the inside of a factory' saying what they thought was best for working-class women.[21] She claimed that as a trade unionist, she knew better than them what working-class women needed.

A year later, she was embroiled in another disagreement with Labour Women. One delegate at the 1933 Labour Women conference suggested that the Means Test was 'tending to reduce the health and stamina of the people, developing a low standard of morality and causing social degeneracy'. Ellen, uncharacteristically measured in her response, asked for the deletion of the clause, and rejected the charge that the working class had a low standard of morality. Indeed, she argued, she was 'amazed at the way the working class of the country had stood up to the awful effects of unemployment'.[22] The mover of the resolution was not happy, censured her for procedural irregularities and accused her of having the 'wrong attitude'. Nevertheless, the offending sentence was deleted.

Ellen was combative and a feisty little fighter but she was no humourless dogmatist and her articles were refreshingly free of jargon. In a somewhat tongue-in-cheek article, entitled 'If I were Chancellor', in the *Daily Express*, she set out her ideas. First of all, she would put as much money as possible into the hands of the poorest; secondly she would abolish all cuts in benefits and salaries; thirdly she would increase state salaries and finally she would give a substantial allowance to low-waged families. She beseeched people to spend, spend, spend, as otherwise civilisation would crack under the weight of goods it could not consume. 'Money', she insisted, 'is a creatable commodity based on public confidence' and did not have magical powers of its own. Inflation held no fears for her. The word itself, *inflation*, she believed, 'gives people fits', so there was a need to invent a different name. Light-heartedly she insisted that 'a woman Chancellor might be useful. A sex that has invented exactly 73 different names for a colour their mothers called 'fawn' would not be beaten for the lack of a soothing synonym.'[23] A year later, in April 1933, Ellen continued with this same theme, this time pointing to the vast and unused deposits of cash in banks which could be used to stimulate the economy.

Communism and Party Tensions

Ellen's naturally rebellious and dissident temperament, no longer bound by parliamentary decorum, was now uninhibited. Although no longer a member of the official Communist Party she joined communist-led organisations and agreed with much Communist Party propaganda. In company with many on the left, she ignored the voices of those warning of what was going on in the Soviet Union. Throughout this period, Ellen was repeatedly in trouble with the Labour Party for not conforming to party discipline. In October 1933 at the Labour Party conference, 'many delegates clamoured for her expulsion from the party for allegedly "coquetting with communism". Ellen, denied a chance to reply, left in a rage.'[24] In October 1934, the Party committee proposed expelling anyone connected with the communist-fronted Relief Committee for the Victims of Fascism to which Ellen belonged.[25] She resigned from the Committee.

No longer an MP, Ellen now demanded that the class war be fought outside Parliament, particularly given the Conservative-dominated National government's majority. Unabashed by Labour's ban on the Relief Committee she once again joined forces with the Communist Party and supported its tactic to set up a National Unemployed Workers' Movement. This communist-front organisation organised hunger marches as a way of fighting back against rising unemployment and the increasing desperation of the poor and the vulnerable. There were many hunger marches, all led by Communists, but the Labour Party opposed them because they feared that such marches undermined Parliament. At the Labour Party annual conference in 1934 Ellen rounded on the NEC for missing 'a magnificent opportunity when they did not take over the whole question of the hunger march and mass protest against the Unemployment Bill'.[26] At the conference, she pleaded with the Executive to do something for the poorest areas: 'we should not keep our eyes focused too much on things 25 years hence, but on the men, women and children who are starving now and have been for ten years.'[27] Ellen's emotional tirade would resound well outside conference but she was politically acute enough to realise that the Labour Party, weakened by the catastrophic defeat of 1931, was not in a position to change the law and was certainly not going to be part of a campaign dominated by the Communist Party.

Towards Parliament Again

In 1932, Ellen Wilkinson was selected as Labour candidate for Jarrow, a north-east ship-building town. She was glad to have a constituency to nurture. In a letter to Winifred Holtby she mentioned having to drive a friend, whose child had chickenpox and whose husband had quincy, between London and Guildford each day. Ellen wrote that she much preferred the long drive to Jarrow because it was much 'easier than driving a car on the Guildford Road ... I'd rather cope with a crisis in the world's affairs than one mess of dishes on a cottage sink, wouldn't you? Or am I utterly depraved?'[28]

Jarrow and its people suited 'Red Ellen': here was a town, a cause and a population she could fight for. In the early 1930s it was one of the most disadvantaged and depressed towns in England. The

Jarrow shipyard had been taken over by a consortium backed by the Bank of England which immediately closed and then demolished it. Ellen described how oxyacetylene burners destroyed the steel girders, cranes crashed to the ground, machine shops emptied, blast furnaces and chimneys destroyed. She wept at the death of Jarrow's great shipyard. In her view, the closing of the shipyard, the resulting huge increase in unemployment and the reluctance of the coalition government to help the industrial north were symptoms of a national evil and of the wastefulness of capitalism. She thought that the attitude of the government to the plight of the northeast was 'simply damnable'. The government, she maintained, turned down one thing after another, it turned down the shipyard and it turned down the steelworks. 'What do they propose to do about Jarrow?' she pleaded.

In January 1934 Ellen organised a deputation of about 400 men and 50 women to meet Ramsay MacDonald when he visited his Seaham constituency, only a few miles away from Jarrow. The demonstrators, hungry and ill-shod, marched in gale-force winds to protest about the proposed dismantling of the Jarrow shipyard.[29] Ellen and a few others were invited to meet the Prime Minister. 'It was always difficult', she remarked, 'to resist MacDonald when he himself had determined to be charming. I tried hard to be unimpressed ... to remember what this man had done to the movement that alone could help these men and women'.[30] Ellen, though beguiled by the Prime Minister's smooth words and charm, remained convinced about the need for change. At best, the deputation had given hope to the people of Jarrow, hope that someone had listened to them, hope to carry on the struggle in order that something might eventually be done. Moreover, she noted, the publicity given to the event brought the plight of Jarrow to public notice. 'Jarrow', she said, 'began to be news'.

Towards the end of 1934, the government passed the Special Areas (Development and Improvement) Act which nominated certain regions, including Jarrow, 'Special Areas', and provided about £2 million to help their revival. It was too little and too late. In Ellen's opinion the Special Areas scheme advantaged employers rather than the workers. Under the scheme employers were not only offered cheap land, subsidised factories, new roads and other services but they paid no local taxes and had their income tax bill considerably reduced. As she complained, there were no Means Test for employers, and no inquiry made as to whether the firm needed public assistance from the government. The result, she raged, was 'colossal waste ... waste of men, waste of intelligence, waste of physical strength, waste of invaluable national assets'.

In 1935 Ellen had another chance to make a difference. For her, the most maddening thing about being out of Parliament was that she 'lost the influence for helping others and for fighting new causes'. With renewed optimism and with a new seat to contest she threw herself into the November 1935 General Election. At this point, Ellen asserted that she was a firm believer in parliamentary democracy. 'I want Socialism in this country as quickly as we can get it, but I also believe in the traditions of this country and in Parliamentary Government ... I believe our British principles of Parliamentary democracy are still the best yet formulated anywhere in the world.' In a leaflet entitled 'A Vote for the Conservatives is a Vote for Despair' she criticised the Conservative-dominated government for financing industry in the south and neglecting the interests of northern constituencies. The government, she accused, 'has done nothing to check this great move South which is draining the life-blood of the North'.

Electioneering she found exciting. There was, in Ellen's opinion, nothing in the world like the 'sound and smell of an election committee-room, bare of everything but trestle tables, election charts and bundles of electioneering propaganda'. She enjoyed campaigning on the streets once more, still happy to hop on to borrowed kitchen chairs to talk to women who would never attend a more formal political meeting. She worked hard in her new constituency, stopping only to cook hasty meals in her committee rooms, using a biscuit-tin lid as a frying pan. Ellen Wilkinson was in a strong position. The Jarrow electorate, affronted by the government's attempts to stop a new steel plant being built there, were reluctant to vote Tory. Over 85 per cent of the electorate voted and she won convincingly, converting a previous Conservative majority of 3,192 into a Labour one of 2,350. 'Is there any thrill', Ellen commented, 'quite like that moment after winning a hard-fought election contest?'

The 1935 General Election held on 14 November ushered in a new Parliament, one that would sit for a further ten years until the end of the Second World War. The Conservative Party once again dominated: the Tories won 386 seats, the Liberals 21 seats, National Labour 8 seats, National Liberals 33. Labour gained 154 seats, an increase of 102 over the previous election but still too small to make much of a difference. Nine women were returned to Parliament: six Conservatives, one Liberal, one Independent, and one Labour – Ellen Wilkinson. Once again, she was the only woman on the Labour benches. But to her great delight, Ramsay MacDonald lost his seat in the election and his party, National Labour, was crushed.

5

Fighting Fascism and Imperialism in the 1930s

Throughout Europe, fascists were gaining in strength. For Ellen this was an abomination and she spent much of the 1930s challenging them. In her view, it was no use denouncing fascism as a 'load of rubbish' unless 'one can substantiate with solid criticism and knowledge'. She wanted to curb the tendency for 'fascism' to become 'a portmanteau word, useful to include every sort of thing the speaker happens to dislike'. And so, with the German communist Edward Conze, she co-authored a book analysing the reasons for fascism and its popularity, favouring a Marxist analysis to explain it. 'When economic breakdown becomes a terrifying reality, when to the hunger and despair of the workers is added the ruin of the middle classes,' they argued, fascism rears its head.[1] Created by Benito Mussolini in 1919, fascists came to believe in the supremacy of one national or ethnic group, held democracy in contempt and insisted on obedience to a powerful demagogic leader. Fascism, the co-authors claimed, inevitably led to war because its leaders wanted to take land and resources from other countries. In their opinion fascism was as much a failure of the left to provide leadership as a success of the fascists to provide new political ideas. The authors maintained that Marxist parties did not offer an adequate alternative, were too organisationally chaotic, too impractical and too fond of using off-putting language. 'What exactly did "ideological capitulation before the bourgeoisie" mean to the ordinary worker?' they asked.

The Advance of Fascism in Germany

Ellen was worried that 'in Germany, as in Italy, Poland, Hungary and elsewhere, dictatorship has usurped the place of democracy.

Persecution and terror have overthrown freedom of speech and freedom of the Press. Religious and racial intolerance in its vilest form has reappeared.' Many like her thought that Germany, which suffered a humiliating defeat in the First World War, was a fertile place for the growth of fascism. A crushed nation, economic collapse, a scapegoated minority, fragile government and a suppressed left-wing were, she argued, ingredients for impending disaster. One of Germany's major grievances was the harshness of the Treaty of Versailles which the Allies had imposed on the conquered Germany. Ellen was not alone in thinking the treaty much too punitive. When Germany was hit by the Great Depression, banks collapsed, unemployment rose to nearly 30 per cent and the Nazis, who unjustly blamed the Treaty of Versailles and the Jews for everything, grew in power.

Reviled by the Conservatives in England and fascists in Germany, Ellen was a darling of the German left. In July 1932, she was invited to Germany to help the socialists in the coming General Election. She was told that

the elections will, I fear be terroristic, at least in the rural areas ... Hitler is a travelling showman with a booming voice and inwardly so paralysed by dark fears and apprehensions that he is totally incapacitated except when he can boom away. His booming has filled both himself and his hearers with a pretentious bravura that carries him and them into a drunken ecstasy of sadistic revivalism.[2]

Socialists, she was warned, were in danger of being beaten up. 'It was this fear that decided me to go', she scribbled on her letter of invitation. And newly out of Parliament, she now had the time.

Ellen learned German for three months, carried an anti-fascist flag and brought letters of support from the Labour Party and the TUC. Her audiences were told that fascists talked peace but intended war, preached freedom but oppressed, promised social justice but plotted class-domination. 'We have seen', she wailed, 'how you have striven to stem the turbulent, ever-rising flood of Fascist reaction ... Capitalism has failed. Socialism alone can save the world.'[3] Predictably, the elections took place in an atmosphere of brutality and persecution with the result that the Nazi Party grew more powerful in the Reichstag. Ellen returned to England downcast.

In January 1933, Hitler became Chancellor of Germany and called for new elections. Six days before they took place, on the night of 27 February, the German Parliament, the Reichstag, was set on fire: a lone Dutchman, the former communist Van der Lubbe, was discovered on the premises. The Nazis, keen to uncover Soviet complicity, accused him and the Communist Party of torching the building. As soon as the Reichstag had burned down, Ellen reported, Nazi leaders announced that a real terror would begin and with it the systematic hunting down of every socialist, every communist, every Jew and every left-leaning intellectual. The *Daily Herald* published her horrific accounts of how leading socialists, such as the Deputy of the Reichstag and the ex-Minister of the Interior, had their houses broken into and everything breakable smashed, how they were arrested and taken to a prison where the Nazis 'amused themselves by doing all the things they could think of – and they had unpleasant minds – finishing by giving a quarter litre of castor oil'. Berlin, she maintained, was a city in which everybody was afraid.

Four leading communists, as well as Van der Lubbe, were charged with setting fire to the Reichstag. At once Ellen sprang into action. She was aware that international pressure was crucial if the accused were to be given any chance of a fair trial so she invited a number of leading anti-fascists from all political parties to her tiny flat. Soon, a Relief Committee for the Victims of German Fascism was formed to mobilise world opinion.

During the summer months of 1933, Ellen helped plan 'The Legal Commission of Enquiry into the Burning of the Reichstag'. This mock trial was part of an anti-fascist protest movement that aimed to focus international attention on the events in Germany by examining the evidence. It had no legal status but, as Ellen remarked, they wanted to judge the German government at the 'bar of world opinion' and to put pressure on the judges in the Nazi trial due two weeks later. On Wednesday, 6 September, Winifred Holtby wrote to Lady Rhondda:

> Ellen Wilkinson has just left. She has been here to supper. I gather that before Monday she must arrange for (a) hospitality (b) an

official reception (c) accommodation at the Law Courts (d) a press – for an international committee of distinguished jurists, about to sift the Reichstag Fire evidence ... Too, too, tiresome, as she has now all the arrangements to do – has been haring about the continent without sleep for ninety-six hours. ... Life, my dear, Goes On, as they say. The spate of treason, mutiny, arson and whatnot that has flowed through this room tonight fairly makes the atmosphere hum.[4]

Knowing that it would lend legal authority to the trial, Ellen booked the Law Society Court Room for the Enquiry. When the Nazi government heard about these arrangements it tried to prevent it taking place. Prince Bismarck, the German Charge d'affaires, called in on the Foreign Office to protest that the trial was held 'for propaganda purposes and constituted flagrant intervention in the internal affairs of Germany'. The German government, he insisted, would hold 'H.M. Government responsible for its being allowed to take place and for acquiescing in such unwarranted interference in German affairs'. Bismarck 'earnestly hoped that all these meetings could and would be stopped, as he feared the effect in Germany would be very bad and Anglo-German relations would be still further impaired.'[5] The Foreign Office (FO) informed him that it was impossible to stop either the 'trial' or the meetings, as both were legal. In private, the FO tried to pressurise the Law Society to cancel Ellen's contract for the Court Room but they refused to do so. The FO also kept an eye on her through the Special Branch who furtively attended meetings of the Reichstag Trial Committee.[6]

Ellen and the Committee, aware that any hint of political intrigue might undermine the credibility of the trial, deliberately kept the Enquiry proceedings formal, rigorous and legalistic. Between 14 and 18 September the celebrated British barrister and eminent Labour Party member, D.N. Pritt and his international legal team, heard detailed evidence about the fire and the Nazi reaction to it. Several leading German politicians, writers and officials who were now refugees gave evidence. One witness (the former President of Police in Berlin who had had responsibility for Reichstag security) testified that the Nazis must have helped place the incendiary material in the building. The judges concluded that Van der Lubbe was not a member of the Communist Party but an opponent of it; that the accused communists were all innocent; that Van der Lubbe could not have acted alone; and that the Reichstag was set on fire by Nazi leaders. Press coverage was wide and, as Ellen had hoped, electrified anti-Nazi sentiment.

Meanwhile, in Germany, Nazi newspapers demanded the death penalty for anyone who gave evidence in support of the accused. Surprisingly, the German court, which was put on the defensive by the adverse publicity generated by the Legal Commission in London, acquitted and eventually released four of the defendants. Van der Lubbe was found guilty and was executed on 10 January 1934 – Ellen called it 'judicial murder'. For the moment, the communist leaders were safe. However, shortly afterwards, a very angry Hitler announced that all future treason trials would be held in a new Nazi-dominated People's Court. It marked the end of any legal justice in Germany.

The Labour Party and the Fascist Threat

Herbert Morrison, one of the leading figures in the Labour Party, shared Ellen Wilkinson's concern about the imminent dangers of fascism and both wanted to fight it. They just differed over strategy. The former was keen to keep the Labour Party separate and distinct whereas the latter, as ever, wanted to overcome political boundaries and liaise with those who shared her fear about the advance of fascism. In the past, Ellen had successfully worked with women from across the political spectrum – Tories, Independents and Liberals – and proposed embarking on similar liaisons with those on the extreme left. Herbert Morrison disagreed. He (rightly) suspected that the League Against Fascism was yet another communist front – there were nine Communists among the 42 members of the Committee – and in September 1934, placed it on the banned list of organisations. The NEC followed by sending warning letters to Labour Party members.[7] Ellen duly resigned from the League but continued to help in its campaigns, and joined other newly-named communist-front organisations until they too were banned.

Ellen's growing international reputation was not matched with acclaim in the Labour Party. At the 1933 Labour Party conference she faced a number of criticisms. First of all delegates accused her of misusing money collected for German political refugees by giving it to communist groups. She denied the charge. Secondly, Ellen Wilkinson was rebuked by Herbert Morrison. In his pamphlet *The Communist Solar System*, Morrison drew up a list of proscribed organisations and Wilkinson belonged to a number of them. Characteristically, she defended her membership. In a debate about communists and their role in the Labour Party, the two confronted each other. She accused Morrison of 'going on the defensive', and said that *The Communist Solar System* was 'a magnificent advertisement of the energy and drive of the Communist Party in this country. Why have those organisations flourished like this? Because our own Executive has not acted quickly enough.' Ellen condemned the Labour Party for leaving the Reichstag Fire trial, and with it the defence of democracy, in the hands of an unofficial Committee. Labour, she insisted, should have taken the lead. In reply, Morrison argued that Miss Wilkinson's

energy and drive go into wrong channels and sometimes she is a bit of a nuisance to us ... instead of running straight over and starting an unofficial organisation in association with people whom she knows she ought not to associate with ... she would be better occupied by concentrating her undoubted energy and drive on the forward work of the Party.[8]

There was a flirtatious edge to their exchanges that was not lost on many of the delegates.

A number of German communists and socialists who wanted to flee Germany turned to Ellen for help. She gave her money from journalism to German Jewish émigrés,[9] put others up in her flat and tried to help refugees by publicising their plight. She was anxious about the 'unconscious growth of anti-semitism' in the UK, speaking of casual conversations she had overheard, such as: 'it is terrible the number of Jews one sees about nowadays. The country is overrun with them.' It was this type of atmosphere, she said, that spread through the world like 'an all-pervasive gas' and made it harder for refugees to be welcomed.

At the 1934 Labour Party conference she protested that the Home Secretary, who had allowed right-wing refugees to enter, had closed 'the gates of England to political refugees from Fascism'.[10] In an article for the *Daily Herald* entitled 'No Home, No Country, No Hope' Ellen condemned the UK for being the most inhospitable country for refugees, and for imposing restrictions in a way that no other country bordering on Germany was doing. She had one small triumph when she persuaded the Home Secretary to allow the remaining communist members of the Reichstag into England. Sadly, some refugees, like her friend Dora Fabian, were threatened and sometimes murdered by Nazis agents operating in England.

Political action was combined with humanitarian relief. Most of Ellen's efforts were concentrated in the Saar, helping refugees, mostly from the working class, with food and lodging.[11] She helped set up a children's home for the children of Nazi victims and led a campaign to adopt children who had lost parents in often horrendous circumstances. She even helped persuade a reluctant Home Secretary to allow German refugee children into the country and guaranteed funding to support them: the descendants of at least 150 children have Ellen Wilkinson and her colleagues to thank for their lives.

In her newspaper articles, probably using information provided by her German refugee friends, Ellen continued to describe the increasing violence and anti-semitism in Germany. One article told of how Albert Einstein had his Berlin house damaged, his books scattered and his manuscripts and notebooks destroyed. He was lucky. For less prominent individuals, she reported, the treatment was worse. The Nazis' 'first attention to their Jewish prisoners is to smash their noses ... at one time they broke into a Jewish café, took away 4 people whom they beat unconsciously and compelled them to lick each other's wounds and the blood on the table when they regained consciousness'. Fascism, Ellen declared, meant terror. 'It means hitting your opponent hard and not merely killing them but torturing them.' She had herself heard the awful screams of human beings in agony and had witnessed lorry-loads of armed thugs dragging people out of their houses and beating them. Ellen told of whips made of steel springs, 'bone-breaking instruments which tore flesh and skin' and of rubber truncheons which burst internal organs but left no mark on the outside. In her view, 'the contempt for civil order, for personal rights, for constitutional methods of change' was slowly engulfing Europe 'like a thick black wave of despair'. Bullies, she insisted, ruled in Germany.

The Nazis, Ellen wrote in *Time and Tide*, had no use for women outside the home. Under Hitler's orders women were dismissed from their posts in universities, from law practices, from hospitals and doctors' surgeries and all public services. She reported how one Nazi officer strode into a university exam hall to make sure there were no Jews and socialists there, adding 'and the women may as well go too. Law exams won't help them bear better children'. The wholesale clearance from public services of Germany's most active and devoted women, she cried, was an all-absorbing tragedy for feminists. Paradoxically, she noted, gender difference did not apply to Jewish women, who were given equality with Jewish men, i.e. they were not immune from the 'sickening Nazi savagery'. Nazi newspapers denounced her as a 'Jew of the Jews'. And when the British ambassador to Berlin suggested to Hermann Goering, the founder of the notorious Gestapo, that he visit Britain he was told: 'If I came to London all your Ellen Wilkinsons would throw carrots at me.'[12]

Towards War

In the early grey hours of Friday, 14 February 1936 Ellen, once more an MP, stepped into an aeroplane at Hendon for a covert journey to Germany. She had been banned from the country and was in danger of arrest, expulsion or worse if she was discovered. The *Sunday Referee* had sent her on a mission to find out what was happening in the Rhineland, 'behind the smoke screen of propaganda set up by Goebbels', to find out Germany's plans for war and 'tear down the mask of geniality the Nazis have assumed during the Olympic Games'.

In her newspaper article, telephoned from under a pile of bedclothes to prevent her voice being heard, she reported that the grip of Goering's secret police had tightened, that even more people had been arrested and still more were frightened to speak out. Everywhere in Berlin, Ellen wrote, people talked of war. We are nearer the abyss, she reported, than we know. In a clandestine interview with an unnamed German minister Ellen discovered that the Germans had a detailed plan to move their troops to the Rhine. 'France would scream', said the Minister, 'but she dare not mobilise without England. And can you imagine England moving to stop us moving our (German) troops within our own country?' As soon as she had filed her report about the remilitarisation of the Rhine she began packing her suitcase. Ellen broke the story on 16 February 1936 under the headline 'Hitler Prepares to March on Rhine'. She was the first correspondent to write about it. A few weeks later, on 7 March 1936, Hitler's troops marched into the Rhineland breaking the terms of the Treaty of Locarno which Germany had signed voluntarily. 'All over Europe', she cried, 'there are thousands of desperate people praying, against hope, against bitter experience, that something will be done'.

Ellen condemned the British government for being too friendly with the German ambassador. 'At how many dinner parties given in London where Herr von Ribbentrop was present, in how many aristocratic houses', she asked in the House of Commons, 'had the mood been indicated that of course we do not want to stand in the way of Germany, and that if Germany takes Austria there will be no question of any fighting?'[13] Later, she criticised the upper classes for wielding so much control over foreign affairs. 'I understand the materialistic conception of history, but would like to write a dietetic conception of history, because so much of British foreign policy is decided at swell dinner parties.'

Ellen condemned Neville Chamberlain for 'putting the narrow interests of his class ... and of the rich, before the national interests.'[14] He was, she insisted, 'not the man to lead the country'. Chamberlain's whole soul, she claimed, was with the fascists, and accused him of taking Britain towards fascism.[15] She launched her most vitriolic attack on Chamberlain when he signed the Munich Agreement, permitting Germany to annex the Sudetenland, an area in Czechoslovakia. In September 1938 Ellen spoke to a crowd of nearly 40,000 people in Trafalgar Square at a Save Peace Demonstration saying of Neville Chamberlain: 'We don't trust you.

We believe that you went to Germany to fix up a sale of the liberties of Czechoslovakia.' When Hitler marched into the rest of the country six months later she called it the rape of Czechoslovakia.

In Ellen's opinion, Nazi invasions could be stopped. She criticised the French and British leaders for not saying 'No' to Hitler. Never once, she pointed out, had the Nazi leader taken a step of aggression until he knew that he would not be opposed by Britain and France. 'We had to say No now or it would be too late.' In her opinion the dictators, namely Mussolini, Hitler and Hirohito, would not act aggressively towards another nation without being sure that the UK would not intervene. Before Japan invaded Manchuria, before Mussolini invaded Abyssinia and before Hitler invaded Austria, feelers were put out to ascertain public opinion. She believed that Britain made Hitler's path easy. The politics of the British government, she suggested, read like the *Decline and Fall of the British Moral Empire*.[16]

The Advance of Fascism in Spain

Just as importantly, Ellen Wilkinson helped Spanish socialists to fight against the encroachment of fascism: in November 1934 she and Lord Listowel were thrown out of Spain for their activities. They had been visiting the country as representatives of the Relief Committee for Victims of Fascism. A month before their visit, an uprising of miners had led to the foundation of a socialist republic at Oviedo, Asturias, in northern Spain. Troops under General Franco were brought in from north Africa, to quell the Republic. Looking pale after travelling continuously for two days and two nights, Ellen reported that army repression had been brutal and there had been victimisation on a terrible scale. The miners, she said, had fled to the hills leaving their wives and children behind. African, Arab and Moroccan troops, 'maddened with drink had been let loose in the first terrible days after the miners' surrender', doing things that no Spanish soldier would dare do.[17] The Spanish government responded by arresting every journalist who wanted to report it. That, Ellen maintained, was why she went there.

The army was in control of Oviedo when Ellen and Lord Listovel arrived. As soon as they made a public appearance, the two were confronted with an indignant and hostile crowd who booed and whistled and threw things at them. They were advised to leave the region under escort. Ellen claimed that the crowd had been orchestrated as a pretext to get rid of them commenting that 'I have faced enough hostile crowds in Britain as suffragist, and as parliamentary candidate, to know when a crowd is really dangerous.' The two were bundled into a car 'for protection' and driven for over 17 hours to the Spanish border. Ellen insisted that they had been kidnapped.

Critics claimed that their trip was badly conceived, ill-timed and harmful to Spanish socialists. The *Daily Express* maintained that 'the Spaniards should not have allowed these British Nosey Parkers to stay as long as they did'. A Labour Party member, who lived in Spain, wrote to Labour Party headquarters complaining that Ellen and Listowel were giving the party a bad name in Spain. In his letter he stated 'I think that this visit was very badly conceived and much worse in its execution ... Personally I think they only came to have a joy ride at other peoples' expense and then be able to return to England and talk about it and get fees for lecturing.'[18] Officials agreed with his sentiments and Ellen nearly faced disciplinary action by the Labour Party and NUDAW for her actions.

In 1936 her support for Spanish socialists was further tested. In February the Popular Front, a coalition of radical groups, was elected in Spain. The new government immediately released all political prisoners, introduced land reforms, restored Catalan autonomy, banned the fascist Falange Party and transferred right-wing military leaders like Franco to posts outside the country. At once Spanish army officers plotted against the democratically elected government and in July 1936 civil war broke out. Ellen, who believed that the civil war was part of an international struggle against fascism, argued that military help should be given to defend the government. Neville Chamberlain thought otherwise and hid behind the principle of non-intervention. To its discredit, the Labour leadership and the TUC, fearing that intervention might precipitate a European war, took Chamberlain's side.

Ellen remained in a minority within the Labour Party but she was joined by some powerful men. Herbert Morrison, perhaps influenced by Ellen, was one of the first of the Labour Party's more established figures to denounce non-intervention and urge support for the Spanish legitimate government. At an NEC meeting in January 1937 he proposed that Labour put pressure on the National government to allow the Spanish government to buy arms. The motion was defeated. By now, Morrison shared Wilkinson's dismay and despair. He was equally disturbed that a constitutionally elected government had been overthrown by the army and urged the British government to help Spanish democracy. It was perhaps a turning point in their relationship. However, although the two agreed about Spain they still differed on political strategy. Ellen continued to work across party lines, joined communist-fronted organisations and tried to get the Labour Party to join United Front campaigns, whereas Herbert Morrison held stubbornly to the idea of keeping the Labour Party separate from other organisations.

Providing humanitarian aid was perhaps Ellen's most crucial service to the Spanish government. In 1936 she had helped set up the Spanish Medical Aid Committee as well as a Parliamentary committee for Spain to help those in need of food and clothing; and she was a founder member of the National Joint Committee for Spanish Relief which co-ordinated the work of the various groups helping Republican Spain. In April 1937 she travelled to Spain with a cross-party section of women, Eleanor Rathbone, the Duchess of Atholl and Dame Rachel Crowdy on behalf of the National Joint Committee for Spanish Relief. In Barcelona they were welcomed by the Spanish Republican government keen to gather as much support from England as it could. They visited Valencia and met the Republican leader Dolores Ibarruri, known as La Passionaria, who Ellen acknowledged was 'filled with such courage, ardour, and nobility of spirit that she inspired everyone'.

In Madrid, she reported that 'shells from rebel six inch guns, smashing in the street outside, tearing through the roof of a theatre blew mangled bodies of women and children' through the doorway of the hotel where she was lunching with the other members of the delegation. Their car was standing nearby. Before they could drive away, the body of one of the victims had to be wiped off it; a gruesome reminder of the reality of war. These experiences made an impact on all four women and they returned with a new commitment to organise relief schemes and convince the British government that Franco and his army were being assisted by German and Italian forces. One of their notable successes was persuading the government to allow nearly 4,000 Basque children to come to Britain as refugees. Ellen was successful in getting her union, NUDAW, to raise a voluntary levy for a period of three months to help finance it. Soon people were calling Ellen the 'pocket Passionara'.

Shortly after her return from Spain, Guernica was bombed by the German air-force. On Thursday 8 May, identifying with the fate of the Republicans and frustrated by parliament's reluctance to do anything to help, Ellen broke down and sobbed during a debate on Spain in the House of Commons. The bombing of Guernica in April 1937 changed the Labour Party's attitude towards the Spanish government. It denounced the bombing as an 'outrage upon humanity, as a violation of the principles of civilisation, and a manifestation of the merciless and inhuman spirit' of the Nazis and fascists.[19]

The Special Branch was still taking a keen interest in Miss Wilkinson and it reported on a speech she made at a demonstration held on Sunday, 13 June 1937 in Trafalgar Square. According to the Special Branch report, Ellen had claimed that the British National government was morally responsible for the mass murder taking place in Spain. The report alleged that she had accused the government of 'being fascist in outlook' and had reproached it for rendering the fullest possible support to Franco when it refused 'to allow the legally established Spanish Government to purchase arms for the maintenance of law and order in Spain'. Two civil servants annotated the report saying: 'Miss Ellen Wilkinson made a number of untrue statements; otherwise it must have been a very boring meeting.' Another added: 'Miss Ellen Wilkinson seldom makes anything but untrue statements either from ignorance or sheer bad luck.'[20]

At the next Labour Party conference Ellen's analysis of the situation in Spain was now, at last, accepted. The Labour Party, horrified by Guernica and embarrassed by its position of non-intervention, reversed its policy, advocated supplying arms to the Republic and organised a series of mass demonstrations in support of the Spanish government. In October 1937 the NEC set up a Spain Campaign

Committee to further its aims: Ellen, along with William Gillies, was elected Joint Secretary. The Committee immediately organised an intensive publicity campaign, using the same traditional method of persuasive protest that the young Ellen had used in her suffragist days. Public meetings and demonstrations were held; organisations were encouraged to pass resolutions demanding the end of 'Non-Intervention'; letters and telegrams were sent to MPs and to the government; the press were bombarded with propaganda; and posters were plastered around towns and cities. The campaign began on 14 November 1937 at the Free Trade Hall in Manchester where over 3,000 people packed in to hear Ellen Wilkinson speak. And yet more demands were made on her time and energies as organisers used her celebrity appeal to attract audiences.

Immediately, the Campaign Committee appealed for 'Freedom, Food and Justice and the ending of Fascist intervention'. Franco, they maintained, 'is a rebel. His troops are invaders. His ships are pirates … The war in Spain is an international war … We are not neutrals in this conflict. We have never been neutrals; we will never be neutrals; we cannot be neutrals.'[21] The Committee called for the immediate withdrawal of foreign troops in Spain and insisted that the legitimate government be allowed to purchase weapons. After battles with her colleagues and many threats of expulsion, Ellen's views of Franco and the fascists were accepted by the Labour Party.

In December 1937 the NEC authorised Ellen Wilkinson and Clement Attlee to visit Spain to give encouragement to the troops fighting on the government side. It was a demanding tour, full of incident. In Barcelona the two stayed with the Prime Minister, Negrin, before being driven to Madrid. Here they visited the frontline trenches under artillery fire and carried out an inspection of the British Battalion of the International Brigade. They visited a school where working-class children were as 'keen as needles, but so thin, every day they had to come through falling shells or casual bullets to a school only 2½ miles from the trenches'.[22] One day, Ellen saw 1,500 children line up for a cup of milk, dried powder, water and a biscuit.

Starvation threatened to undermine the Spanish government so the main focus of Ellen's work back in Britain was organising humanitarian relief. In Madrid alone there were a million people,

Figure 5.1 Ellen and Clement Attlee inspecting bomb damage
in Madrid, 1937. (People's History Museum, Manchester)

many of them sick and wounded, who faced another winter of war
without sufficient food, of which the most urgent was seen to be lack
of milk. She helped set up the Milk for Spain fund and persuaded
NUDAW and the Co-operative Union to get involved. Customers at
the 20,000 Co-operative shops were encouraged to buy a 6d token
to help towards the purchase of cost-price condensed milk and milk
powder to be sent to Spain. In Barcelona, for example, the fund
served 33,000 glasses of milk and a biscuit each morning to children
on their way to school.

Ellen was fully aware that the Spanish government needed more
than milk and food to win. Everywhere she could, in the House of
Commons, at conferences, public meetings, demonstrations and in

newspaper articles, she spoke of the need for arms. Ellen and Eleanor Rathbone constantly asked questions in the House of Commons about the so-called non-intervention pact, the plight of refugees and the role of Germany and Italy in providing arms to the rebel forces. The Conservative Party, riled by their comments, resorted to the favourite weapon of barracking and, according to *Tribune,* seemed 'to take peculiar delight in jeering at their two women opponents, Ellen Wilkinson and Eleanor Rathbone. Their habits on these occasions are sometimes utterly outrageous.'

In March 1938 the Spain Campaign Committee, of which Ellen was Joint Secretary, issued a manifesto calling for the National government to reverse its weapons ban, allow the legitimate Spanish government to purchase arms and for Britain to abandon its policy of non-intervention. The manifesto strongly criticised the National government for continuing to negotiate with Mussolini and Hitler.[23] Two months later, Ellen Wilkinson, Harold Laski, Stafford Cripps and D.N. Pritt submitted a joint confidential memo to the Executive entitled 'The International Situation'. In their memorandum the four reiterated the dangers to democracy of non-intervention in Spain and criticised Hitler's incursions into Austria, Czechoslovakia and other free states in the area. They accused the National government of being 'effectively pro-Fascist' and of being unconcerned about the destruction of democracy. The only alternative, they argued, was a socialist reconstruction of Great Britain with a primary and vital objective to overthrow the National government. They recommended cooperating with other anti-Government political parties as it 'is better to join forces with anti-Socialist democrats than to see both Socialism and Democracy perish'.[24] Ellen believed that democracy was at stake as the threat of fascism grew. 'We cannot allow the friends of Fascism to remain in power while we quarrel amongst ourselves. We are united in a determination to remove Chamberlain.' All their proposals were rejected.

At the 1938 Labour Party conference, Ellen once more called for the right of the Spanish Government to purchase arms. If the Spanish Government was given the freedom to buy aeroplanes, anti-aircraft guns, artillery and tanks, she urged, Franco's insurgents could not win. In October, at a meeting in London's Queen's Hall, she made a 'characteristically aggressive and informative onslaught on the Government'. Ellen, like other speakers, condemned the foreign policy of the National government, criticised Franco's attack on the lawfully elected Republicans and pleaded with Britain to stop the starvation of the Spanish Republicans. In her view, in the interests of international peace, Franco should be prevented from winning the civil war. If fascism triumphed over democracy, she prophesised, it would mean the consequent destruction of Europe. Ellen was accused in Parliament of recruiting men for the International Brigade, a charge she denied. 'My whole work', she insisted 'has been in helping to provide medical aid and supplies inside Spain and in appealing for money for the wives and dependants of those who have gone to fight'.[25] What else could she have said?

On 1 April 1939 the democratically elected government conceded defeat by Franco's army. Almost immediately, Chamberlain recognised Franco and his fascists as leaders of Spain. The fight was over. Ellen, however, insisted that those who fought to defend Spanish democracy must not be forgotten. At the Labour Party conference that year she moved that conference

> expresses its undying admiration for the heroism of the Spanish people, who, in the face of overwhelming odds, held the Fascist invaders at bay for two and a half years ... retarded the development of Fascist aggression in Europe and helped at least to postpone the outbreak of World War ... The Spanish fight is our fight, because it is a fight against Fascism, and our message from this Conference both to our comrades who lie there and to the men in the concentration camps, and to those men and women whose bodies are being broken in the prisons of Spain, is that we shall not forget. The fight goes on.[26]

Her speech was stirring but even so Ellen and the Spain Committee were criticised by other left-wingers for their political inactivity. Delegates complained that while Franco was massing his troops against Barcelona the Committee was fundraising for the Milk Fund, organising Christmas parcels and issuing Christmas cards and never seriously addressed itself to conducting a political campaign to force the government to abandon its arms embargo. Ellen, used to being attacked by the right-wing of the Labour Party, now found herself the target of criticism from those on the left.

Ellen focused primarily on fighting fascism in Germany and Spain but her commitment to fighting fascism and imperialism led her to speak against it in Austria, Hungary and elsewhere. She once commented that she had 'heard Hitler orate, talked to Gandhi in gaol, picnicked with terrorist leaders on the run in Bengal, lunched with tribal chieftains on the Khyber Pass'. In 1925 she helped set up the Friends of Italian Freedom: she spoke out against Mussolini and later publicised the plight of Abyssinia. In February 1927, she attended the Foundation Congress of the League Against Imperialism in Brussels and helped set up the British section.[27]

It was here that Ellen first met the Indian nationalist Jahawarhal Nehru, later acclaiming him as a 'hero for an heroic age'. She addressed meetings, wrote articles and books, looked after Nehru when he visited England and stage-managed the Parliamentary appearance of Mahatma Gandhi, whom she recognised as a fellow politician with a flair for publicity.[28] Ellen continually condemned the British government's repression in India; she criticised the government's treatment of the Meerut prisoners;[29] she asked uncomfortable questions in the House of Commons about prisoners held in gaol for 20 years as a result of the Lahore Conspiracy;[30] and joined the anti-colonial pressure group, the India League. In August 1932, as part of a delegation of the India League, she visited India for three months, travelling to outlying villages, staying with local people, eating Indian food, meeting both Hindus and Muslims and learning their respective viewpoints.[31] When she returned to England her book, co-written with Krishna Menon, Monica Whately and Leonard Matters, included details of the political repression, torture and starvation which they had encountered on their journey in India. Repression, the authors claimed, forced the spread of terrorist activity.[32]

Meanwhile, the rise of Hitler prompted Ellen to re-evaluate her attitude towards peace. Her experiences in combating fascism in Germany, Spain and elsewhere convinced her that fascism was more dangerous than war and that democracy was worth fighting for. In

September 1936 she resigned from the Peace Pledge Union because she felt utterly unable to leave the United Kingdom defenceless in the face of what was happening abroad. She felt that the peace movement, admirable thought it was, did not fit with the facts of the international situation.[33] In March 1938 Ellen resigned from the Women's International League. On 23 August 1939, Hitler and Stalin signed the Nazi–Soviet Pact in which both countries secretly agreed to invade Poland. The pact, which was defended by the British Communist Party, not only marked the end of Ellen Wilkinson's ideological admiration of communism but of her willingness to work with organisations identified with the British Communist Party.

6

In Parliament Again, 1935–39

I n the 1920s Ellen had worked tirelessly to promote revolution but little by little she relocated her reforming zeal to Parliament. As ever, the contradictory tensions between her beliefs in revolutionary transformation and her recognition of the need for parliamentary pragmatism marked Ellen's life. Despite this, her radical passion continued undiminished. She remained, at least to the communist *Daily Worker*, a 'thorn in the side of the Tories, an inspiration to her own side. Seeing that red-framed head thrown back, chin defiantly out-thrust, hearing that rather harsh, compelling voice it is difficult not to be infected with something of the courage and vitality of one of the most outstanding women of our time.' Yet her spell out of Parliament had made her cautious. So shaken had she been by the loss of her former seat, so dearly did she miss Parliament that she would never again endanger her political career. From now on she would always (in the end and after protest) capitulate when threatened with expulsion from the Labour Party.

In 1935, Ellen was MP for Jarrow, a town with one of the worst unemployment records in England: only 100 out of 8,000 skilled manual workers had work. In her view, the current situation in Jarrow was desperate. 'No one', she protested, 'had a job, except a few railwaymen, officials, the workers in the co-operative stores, and the few clerks and craftsmen who went out of the town to their jobs each day'.[1] The town, she cried, was down and out. She was 'sick of hearing about the sacred rights of private property. I want to hear about the sacred rights of human life.' Once again, stirred by the economic difficulties faced by her constituents, Ellen fought hard to ameliorate some of the worst aspects. One *Star* reporter wrote that he 'met her dog-tired in the small hours; midnight journeys Jarrow, back House, back again Jarrow, speaking, writing, organising, raising funds, steel schemes, Black Areas help, under-fed children, arms orders Germany, victims Fascism, marches, meetings, secret investigating. Whirligig life. Never still.' Her health, never robust, deteriorated further.

First and foremost, Ellen was a local MP dedicated to the needs of her constituents. She held regular surgeries, presented prizes at local schools, attended functions, visited businesses, dealt with individual problems, responded to constituents' letters, and raised issues affecting Jarrow in the House of Commons. In particular, Ellen wanted to remove the power of the government and its agencies to close down shipyards. The closing of the shipyard, she claimed, had 'cut the throat of Jarrow'. On Monday 23 December 1935, just weeks after her election, she led a joint Labour Party and Trades Council demonstration to the Means Test Commissioner. It was a rehearsal for a bigger and better publicised march.

In her election campaign Ellen had pledged to fight for the abolition of the Means Test. When Family Means Testing was first imposed, she had howled 'how can you means test someone without any means?' Ellen saw it as one of the major social injustices of the day and criticised its intrusiveness, the unsympathetic attitude of officials and the inherent shame of having your means tested. As she observed, 'we hear so much about the necessity of providing the capitalist with an "incentive" to go on making profit'.[2] Yet the very same society was shocked when workers declined to find new jobs when the money they earned was used to decrease the income of the rest of their family.

Ellen condemned the Conservative government for paying unemployed people less than they had once received at work. Families were trapped in a vicious circle of low wages, lower benefits and malnutrition, and were punished because a set of greedy capitalists closed down the industry of the town. 'I loathe poverty', she said. 'I don't just mean being hard up and having to do without things for a bit. I mean poverty as an institution, the deep grinding health-destroying poverty in which 70% of the people in this country live.' Her statistics were wildly inaccurate but no one doubted her compassion when she spoke about one Jarrow woman with four children and a sick husband who told her: 'I'm sick of potatoes, potatoes. Some days I buy a cod's head to boil with them to give them a flavour. I pick out the eyes while it's cooking and eat them on a bit of bread. Tasty after so much potato.' In a passionate indictment of the Government she cried that 'poverty at this level is hell'.[3] While the banks were 'stuffed full of money', she complained, 'I am working with men and women who are without'.

With poverty came ill-health and early death. Statistics in the 1930s showed a clear correlation between life expectancy, infant and maternal mortality and poverty, often related to the effects of the 10 per cent cut in benefits. Ellen illustrated the syndrome in this powerful speech to the House of Commons on 8 July 1936:

> I did not notice the occurrence until it became so regular that it became a perfect horror. Every time I got out of the station I was met by some party workers who had always the same story to tell, that a worker in the party had suddenly died … These are cases which it is very difficult to put into statistics, and doctors seldom sign that death is due to starvation or malnutrition. I remember one woman speaking to me and saying that because of the means test she had gone to live with her married son and daughter, who already had four small children. She said 'You know, I do not want to be a burden on them, so I slip out at meal times and say that I have had a bite at my neighbour's.' I remember that case very vividly because the woman died. There was cardiac disease on the certificate but it was obvious the woman was more than half-starved.

Good health, Ellen insisted, was a class question. Deaths in Jarrow from tuberculosis were significantly higher than in some parts of the country because of the effects of unemployment. Ellen was 'blind and sick with rage' at the smug Conservative-dominated National government which had saved £15 million a year through the Means Test at the expense of mothers and babies whose lives she said have been 'as surely sacrificed as if they had been thrown alive into the sea'. In Means Test areas a lack of nutritious food led to higher rates of maternal mortality; lack of nutritious food led to a higher death rate for babies: 200 out of 1,000 babies died, against a national average of 55; a lack of nutrition meant that people in these areas generally died younger than in the rest of the country. Ellen noticed that Jarrow families consumed little milk, and believing that this led to malnutrition and tuberculosis, she persuaded the local authorities to subsidise the provision of school milk in her constituency.

The Jarrow Crusade

In July 1936, aware that all the previous deputations to publicise the plight of Jarrow had failed, David Riley, Chair of the Council, suggested a new strategy: a march of the male unemployed to London. It is highly likely that Ellen had planted the idea in his mind. She had helped plan hunger marches before, ones organised by the Unemployed Workers' Movement, and led by the Communist Party. Only too aware that these communist-inspired marches were easily condemned by trade unions and the Labour Party as far-left propaganda she realised that it was crucial for the Jarrow Crusade to be different if it was to have an impact.

From the beginning the Crusade was carefully stage-managed. For a start, the march was kept non-political and known communists were excluded from it. Ellen kept a deliberately low profile and did most of her work behind the scenes. The march was organised by Jarrow Town Hall, supervised by the Town Clerk, blessed by the local church and supported by the mayor. The marchers chose banners in neutral colours – bold blue letters on a white background – so no political party could claim them. Moreover, all the political parties agreed to bury their partisanship and do what was in the best interests of the whole town.

Ellen was aware of the importance of image. Previous demonstrators were written off as a crowd of bedraggled itinerants so she encouraged the Jarrow marchers to appear as respectable as possible. The marchers, led by David Riley dressed in a suit and bowler hat, looked smart: the men were carefully shaved, broken boots repaired and polished, shabby clothes brushed and mended and waterproof capes rolled neatly over their shoulders. Alcohol was banned. Ellen, using the exemplary organisational skills she had learned from her union days, had left little to chance. The *Guardian* declared that the organisation was 'well-nigh perfect'. She helped raise money for the march which was used to pay for a bus, waterproofs for every man, pocket money, two stamps a week, medical attention, haircutting and shoe-repair facilities. It also helped pay for the thousands of letters sent out by the mayor to trade unions, co-operative societies, local councils and other organisations to raise support for the crusade. Finally Ellen helped find accommodation at night in drill halls, schools, church and town halls and workhouses and used her union connections to ensure that the marchers received a 'cheering welcome' when they marched into towns on the way.

Two hundred men, half of whom were ex-servicemen, were selected and then vetted by the Medical Officer to make sure they were fit and well enough to walk to London. The marchers, many wearing British Legion badges, set off with their MP on Monday 5 October 1936 to walk the 282 miles to London. They planned to arrive in the capital just as the new session of Parliament was opening and present a petition signed by nearly 12,000 Jarrow citizens to the House.

Just before they left, the men attended a short church service and the march was blessed by the Bishop of Jarrow. Shortly after, in a letter to *The Times*, the Bishop of Durham denounced the marchers as a 'revolutionary mob' and put pressure on the Bishop of Jarrow to recant his previous support. Not surprisingly, the letter drew an angry response from Ellen.

She condemned the Bishop for thinking that 'the quiet exercise of our constitutional right to offer a petition to Parliament is dangerous in these days. When constitutional rights are being threatened on every side, democrats should watch vigilantly over rights that have been struggled for and won through centuries of British history'.[4]

In her moving account of the crusade, *The Town that was Murdered*, Ellen charted the progress of herself and the men. She spoke of how the marchers rose at 6.30 a.m. after sleeping on bare boards of a school or other hall – if lucky they had mattresses supplied – or else in the casual ward of a workhouse. Most mornings they were joined by Ellen who had stayed elsewhere, often at the home of a local Labour Party activist or sometimes at the home of a vicar. Each day the men, and Ellen, marched for 50 minutes, rested for ten minutes then marched again. At noon they ate lunch, sometimes stew, tinned fruit and hot tea, and in fine weather took a nap lying on the grass.

When the weather was poor they stood in the rain under their capes, eating sandwiches. Each night there was a meeting at which Ellen normally spoke.

Figure 6.1 Ellen relaxing with the Jarrow marchers. (People's History Museum, Manchester)

Ellen did not walk the whole way and some accused her of 'just dropping in' when she felt the need for a little exercise. However, she walked more miles than most of the other officials, and the men voted her the best woman marcher in England.[5] In fact, Ellen's asthma, bronchial and lung ailments would have been sufficient excuse for her to have left the marching to younger and fitter colleagues, but she never referred to her illness and only left the march for other important business concerning Jarrow. Many times she was in a state of collapse at the end of a day. When she arrived at Market Harborough after a 15-mile hike from Leicester she crumpled with exhaustion.[6] She was scarcely able to talk and was forced to rest before being prescribed a stimulant so that she could speak at an evening meeting.

On one occasion Ellen left the crusade to attend the Labour Party national conference. The Jarrow leaders had asked her 'to arrange a collection and speak about the distressed areas. Imagine if I wasn't there?' she said. 'Why is Miss Wilkinson strolling along the roads instead of proclaiming Jarrow's case?' It was at this conference that Ellen gave one of the most electrifying speeches of her life.

> You cannot expect men trapped in these distressed areas to stay there and starve because it is not convenient to have them coming to London. What has the National Council done? It has disapproved of it. What has gone out from our General Council? Letters saying, in the politest language 'Do not help these men' ... I tell the Executive that they are missing the most marvellous opportunity in a generation ... If you had seen that march from Jarrow you would have realised that it was a great folk movement with everybody there ... I say this to the Party: put yourself at the head of a great movement of moral indignation in this country ... and say 'Our people shall not be starved ... If we cannot do this, what use are we as a Labour Party?[7]

Her speech was not welcomed. Some Conference delegates objected to Ellen's tirade and criticised her for sending hungry and ill-clad men on a long march to London.

Indubitably, the Labour Party did not approve of extra-parliamentary action, particularly because it believed that much of it was still orchestrated by the Communist Party. In later years, Ellen wrote that she had left 'the warm comradeship of the road to an atmosphere of official disapproval'.[8] She was saddened because, whereas the marchers received tea and sympathy from ordinary people in the towns they visited, those expected to be the most compassionate of all, the Labour Party and the trade unions, disapproved. Ellen, upset and angry by the lack of support in her party, insisted that if the Labour Party had put its power behind the crusade the Conservative coalition government might have fallen. There was no doubting Ellen's enormous compassion and untiring energy but statements like this were irrational. In the same breath, she condemned the TUC for accusing the marches as being 'Communist inspired' and for advising trades councils not to help the marchers. This, she later said, led to an odd result in towns such as Chesterfield where the marchers were ignored by the unions and the Labour Party but were given hot meals, help and a place to sleep by the Conservatives.

The Tory press, in sharp contrast to reports on previous hunger marches, wrote sympathetically about the crusade, noting that there were 'friendly feelings shown towards the men during the whole of their long march'.[9] In 1936, the Jarrow marchers received such positive newspaper coverage that the Conservative coalition Cabinet discussed whether journalists could be fed information exposing the origins, motives and 'uselessness' of the Hunger marches in order to discourage the public from giving assistance to them.[10] Fortunately, at the time, newspapers were not umbilically attached to politicians, so continued to portray the marchers benevolently. And ordinary people were significantly more empathetic than the government, the Labour Party or the TUC. At Leicester the Co-operative Society's boot repairers, encouraged by Ellen and the NUDAW, provided the materials and worked all night without pay to repair the worn-out boots of the marching men; in Harrogate the Territorial officers took care of them; in Leeds a newspaper proprietor gave them a meal and free beer; in Barnsley the municipal baths were opened especially for the marchers; in Bedford they were given cigarettes and tobacco by the Rotary Club and sausages by the local butchers;[11] and in Edgware a large and comfortable room at the White Hart Hotel was set ready for the men and Ellen to enjoy a hearty meal of tomato soup, steak and kidney pudding and apple pie, all paid for by the mayor and the Rotary Club.[12]

On 31 October, 30 days and 290 miles later, the crusade reached London where 'heavy rain, driven before a cold north-westerly wind, beat on the backs of the Jarrow marchers'.[13] Ellen wearily remarked that 'we all looked so utterly shabby and weary in our wet clothes that we presented London with the picture of a walking distressed area'.[14]

On 4 November Ellen and the Jarrow marchers tried to present their petition but the Prime Minister refused to meet them.[15] It was a tense moment. Naturally, the tempers of the men rose and some of them called for a sit-in. Eventually the men were persuaded to leave the matter to their MP and a large committee room was booked so that senior figures from the crusade could discuss the situation with politicians from all parties.

When Ellen returned to Jarrow she 'came as near being trampled on. For several minutes nothing could be done as the crowd surged round her, men seized her hands, women smothered her with kisses, children hugged her. Breathless and weary, she beamed happily upon them all.'[16] Yet the Jarrow Crusade failed to gain help for the town and its unemployed. In fact, the situation worsened when the Government initially stopped the marchers' pay because of their unavailability for work. Soon, however, principally because of Ellen's passionate oratory, organisational genius and her bestselling book with that evocative and provocative title *The Town that was Murdered*, Jarrow began to be noticed. The publicity that followed the Jarrow march contributed to the town's renewal and, according to Ellen, did much to raise the question of the relationship between big business and Government. The chief success of the Jarrow marchers, it has been argued, lay in the future. Historians believe that the Jarrow Crusade achieved little of concrete value at the time but 'did, however, shape the post-war perceptions of the 1930s and ensured the attachment of the word "Hungry" to the 1930s in the popular mind'.[17]

Meanwhile, Ellen welcomed help from the Society of Friends who sold cheap seeds, tools and fertilizers to those with allotments. She also thanked the generous benevolence of those who raised money to help the unemployed build a park and a sports stadium and which provided paint and wallpaper for families to redecorate their homes. And when she pleaded for funds to open a nursery school in Jarrow her friend Nancy Astor helped collect the money. However, Ellen insisted that Jarrow did not want charity. They wanted jobs. 'You cannot', she insisted, 'just put a plaster on the wound that is Tyneside'. Eventually, in 1937, largely as a result of the march and their MP's continuous lobbying, new steelworks were built in the town. But Ellen was still not content. In her view, the real revolution would be for British workers to insist on a 'properly planned steel industry for national needs, run in the interests of the community and not to suit the short-term interests of a set of finance-men'.[18]

Ellen and the Left

The 1936 Labour Party conference was a bitter affair for Ellen. She not only witnessed the dismissal of Jarrow's plight but heard of the defeat of the motion to affiliate the Communist Party to Labour and the refusal of Labour to help the legitimate government in Spain. Ellen may have been vociferous about the shortcomings of the Labour Party yet she was silent when her former Russian comrades, Kamenev and Zinoviev, were indicted, trialled and executed in the Soviet Republic on trumped-up charges at around the same time. She even made no comment when the communist *Daily Worker* ran a shocking headline in support of the sentences that read 'Shoot the Reptiles'.

Certainly Ellen was in denial about repression in the Soviet Union and instead was found in the thick of campaigns to affiliate the Communist Party to Labour and to unite the left against fascism. In January 1937 the Socialist League, the Communist Party and the ILP issued a Unity Manifesto that aimed to fight fascism and to persuade the Labour Party to allow the communists into their ranks. Once again, Ellen found herself bound on a trajectory of political self-destruction when she publicly criticised the party for its feeble response to the developing threat of fascism and its unwillingness to unite with other groups. Unfortunately, the term 'United Front' had sinister connotations for the Labour Party and it accused the 'United Front' as being yet another communist attempt to infiltrate and influence the party. *Labour Woman* too was dismissive of such alliances and criticised Ellen's 'lengthy articles' as 'pitched in a somewhat hysterical key'.[19] There was more trouble in store. In yet another heresy hunt the NEC disaffiliated the Socialist League to which Ellen also belonged and banned members of the League from being members of the Labour Party. Later that year the Labour Party conference not only reaffirmed the NEC's decision but declared its intention to expel party members who appeared on the same platform as communists.

Unexpectedly the Party's left-wing was strengthened: Ellen was again elected to the National Executive of the Labour Party, a post she held for most years until she died in 1947. Her re-election to the NEC was a significant step towards greater influence in the party. She was now physically centre stage and would sit on the platform during the Labour Party conferences. At the time, the NEC was in charge of all party organisation, discipline and most importantly, policy. Ellen, as member of the Press and Publicity Department, would write policy documents and thus help shape the course of Labour. The *Daily Express* reported that the 'older lads on the party executive think that the Wilkinsons, the Crippses and the Laskis will be tamed by responsibility now that they are placed at the executive council table'.[20] Indeed, critics have seen Ellen's re-election to the NEC as her first step towards the right. However, as ever, she was on the left leaning side of the Executive, no less outspoken and no more moderate than before.

In January 1937 the first issue of *Tribune* appeared. It had been conceived by Ellen, Aneurin Bevan, Harold Laski, Stafford Cripps and others in response to the disastrous 1936 Labour Party conference where the left had been roundly trounced. In their view, the Labour leadership had betrayed its principles by its seeming indifference to the Jarrow Crusade, means testing, the unemployed, the poor and in its response to the Spanish Civil War and rearmament. There was, she and her colleagues believed, a need for a paper that would act as a conduit for the left's beliefs. Ellen wrote in its first issue, setting the tone for the paper's political direction. In her opinion, half of Britain was in the harsh grip of the Depression, not just the Distressed Areas. 'Any government really alive to the appalling plight of masses of people – suffering from unemployment over long periods, from enforced malnutrition, from abominable housing conditions, from neglect, from despair – would move heaven and earth to bring immediate amelioration.'

Despite setbacks, Ellen never gave up trying to build alliances between the various opposition groups. In April 1938, she was embroiled in yet another Popular Front campaign when she and others on the left put forward a memorandum which urged that Labour form an alliance with liberals, communists and others to fight the next election.[21] It was a reiteration of Communist Party policy. The NEC rejected the memorandum by 17 votes to 4 – only the four MPs who had drafted the proposal voted in support. In January 1939, she found herself once more in a minority and once more in conflict with her party. Again Ellen, and Stafford Cripps, wanted to unite with other left of centre groups to fight the forthcoming election. In their opinion, the Labour Party was unlikely to win a majority so needed the votes of other sympathetic parties, including communists, the

ILP and liberals, to hold office. Cripps resubmitted the memo; again the NEC rejected it. Undeterred, Cripps circulated the memorandum to Labour Party candidates and other affiliated organisations, a gross breach of Labour Party discipline. When the NEC asked him to withdraw his comments and reaffirm his allegiance to the Labour Party Stafford Cripps refused. He was duly expelled by the NEC, in an almost unanimous decision – 18 votes to 1 – from the Labour Party. Only Ellen, 'her chin jutting out, looking defiantly around the table' voted against his expulsion.[22] Ellen insisted that even *if* she disagreed with Stafford Cripps' memo, she would have defended his right to publish it.[23]

Cripps, supported by a number of key figures, led a campaign in support of his actions. This time, neither wishing to resign nor to be thrown out of the Labour Party, Ellen did not join him. She decided to 'remain a loyal member of the Labour Party', resigned from the editorial board of *Tribune* and declined to speak on the same platform as Cripps. Even though she had contributed to the problem by helping to draft the original memorandum, Ellen shared the alarm of other Labour Party members that the Cripps conflict might turn out to be the biggest since the 1931 debacle and feared another damaging schism. Party unity, at that moment, was thought to be more important than political beliefs. Moreover, Ellen did not want to risk her political career for Cripps' seemingly hopeless cause. She was not rich like Stafford Cripps and could not afford to lose her Parliamentary seat again so she moved towards the mainstream of the Labour Party. Nevertheless, some residual loyalty to her old friend was evident at the 1939 NUDAW conference when she urged the Labour Party to reverse its decision about Cripps and allow him back into the Labour Party.

In the long term Ellen wanted to change the world but in the short term she tried to fix the parts that were broken. She once remarked to a female MP 'you can either try some big reform and have a good day till four o'clock', when it failed, 'or you can bring in a minor reform'[24] and be successful. One of her significant achievements was to alleviate the gross injustices of the hire purchase system, and her Act is viewed as one of the few important pieces of social reform passed in this period. For many families the only way to buy furniture or large household appliances was on the 'never-never', that is hire purchase: a system which allowed people to obtain goods immediately and pay for them on a weekly basis.[25] Unfairly, the ownership of the goods remained in the hands of the seller until the final instalment was paid. All too often customers paid twice as much as the goods were worth and were charged extortionate rates of interest. Moreover, if the family missed a payment companies could 'snatch-back' goods without compensation. Allegations of forcible entry, trespass and assault were common especially when many firms employed 'bruisers' to intimidate householders.

Ellen had first brought this problem to the House of Commons in 1930 but at that time was unable to bring her Bill to completion. However, not short of courage and determination, she persuaded, nagged, cajoled, argued, threatened and charmed until she succeeded. By the late 1930s, judges, social workers, the press and other politicians recognised Ellen's vision. Everyone now agreed that it was important to remove the exploitative aspects of the hire purchase system. In 1937, two years after she had been re-elected, and eight years after her first attempt, Ellen brought in another private members' Bill to 'counter the sharp practices of the less reputable hire-purchase traders, whose harrying of the poor was a grave and growing scandal',[26] and to stop 'bruisers' from taking the goods by force. By now, she was more compromising, amending her Bill to accommodate criticisms from the bike and motor trades. And so, in May 1938, the Hire Purchase Act which had had its first reading in 1935, after a very thorough examination and strengthening, and with much goodwill and support from all parties, was given a unanimous third reading. It eventually became law on New Year's Day 1939. Even the Attorney General complimented Ellen for her 'patient and skilful handling of the prolonged negotiations with the various interests concerned'.[27] Ellen's negotiating skills had not only overcome all opposition but she had inadvertently given a boost to an emerging consumer society.

She was less successful with another 'minor' reform. On 21 February 1939 Ellen introduced her Building Societies Bill to protect house owners against jerry-builders. At the time, building societies, in collusion with the builders, offered 95 per cent mortgages on new-build homes but offered no guarantees on quality. Lots of shoddy homes were built and people took out mortgages on them. Ellen's Bill would give purchasers the right to withhold their mortgage repayments if the house was badly built. The Bill was not passed. Instead, the Conservative government passed its own which protected building societies rather than the consumer.

Some historians have come to the strange conclusion that Ellen had abandoned her feminism by the 1930s but her articles and Parliamentary work provide evidence of someone who remained committed to promoting equal opportunities. For example, Ellen insisted that the Depression made things far worse for women. Constant vigilance, she urged, was needed to ensure that the gains fought and won by women were not eroded when life got tough. She continued to work with feminist groups and across party lines to advance women's equality and continued to sponsor Bills, such as the British Nationality and Status of Aliens (Amendment) Bill.[28] In March 1936, she and Nancy Astor, spoke at a packed meeting in Caxton Hall on equal pay for women in the civil service. On 1 April 1936 Ellen introduced a motion to the House of Commons to 'place women in the Civil service on the same scales of pay as apply to men'. Her proposal was surprisingly carried and the government defeated. However, the Prime Minister, Stanley Baldwin, refused to accept the outcome, called for a second vote, and asked that it be treated as a vote of confidence. In the next division, the government won and female civil servants had to wait until 1956 to receive equal pay to men.

By now Ellen had become closer to Herbert Morrison and perhaps they embarked on an affair. Most people disapproved of extra-marital affairs so she was careful to keep any liaison as secret as possible. And yet speculation was rife. The two had much in common when they first met: both were Labour Party members, vegetarians and teetotallers. If, or most likely when, an affair took place both would have been extremely circumspect since any public knowledge of an extra-marital liaison would have meant an end to a political career. In July 1931 Ellen asked Beatrice Webb if it was 'reasonable to expect a woman in public life who did not want to get married to remain celibate if she found a congenial friend who happened to have an uncongenial wife?'[29] Herbert Morrison, known to have an unhappy marriage to a very uncongenial wife, had now become attractive to Ellen. The two may also have been drawn together when they both lost their seats in the 1931 election. It was around this time that Morrison, who worked in a shop as a young man, began writing in the NUDAW journal and speaking at NUDAW conferences. In 1935, Susan Lawrence confided to Beatrice Webb that she would not associate with women indulging in illegitimate affairs, except in the case of old friends like Ellen.[30] We do not know who Lawrence had in mind but maybe she was referring to Wilkinson's relationship with Morrison.

Ellen loved a bit of back-stairs intrigue, and growing ever closer to Morrison, she backed him in his campaign to replace Attlee as leader of the Labour Party. For example, when Attlee was taken ill with prostate trouble and could not attend the opening session of the 1939 Labour Party conference she openly questioned his leadership. She wrote articles in journals and newspapers praising Morrison and hoping that he would be leader soon. In *Time and Tide*, she commented that Attlee's almost total absence from the Conference 'made not the slightest difference,' and went on to say that the man who led the conference on all the main issues was Herbert Morrison. 'Mr Attlee', she reported 'does not command that authority'. Arthur Greenwood, Chair of the NEC, officially deplored the articles and asked Ellen to defend herself. She apparently made a poor show and was lucky to escape official censure. There was a unanimous vote of confidence in Attlee; only Ellen abstained.

Ellen may have modified some of her views in this period but she was no political chameleon and in addition to women's rights, she continued to champion the needs of her Jarrow constituents and her union. She took up individual cases in Parliament such as that of William Haley, aged 16, sentenced to three months' hard labour for the theft of a bicycle. Ellen asked the Home Secretary that 'on account of the boy's extreme youth' he should be taken 'away from prison hard-labour conditions' and given 'more suitable and kindly treatment'.[31] Between 1935 and 1939, she continually challenged the government over its attitudes toward the unemployed, means testing and its ineffectiveness in dealing with the Depression. She asked questions in Parliament about the iron and steel works at Jarrow, equal pay for women civil servants, help for the unemployed, maternity and child welfare, malnutrition and married women's property. And she asked lots of questions about Spain. In 1937 alone Ellen took part in all the key debates about Jarrow, the iron and steel industries, the depressed areas, merchant shipping, old age and widows' pensions, the arms industry, factories, education, milk, agriculture and finance Bills. She asked whether Parliament could have a guarantee that the 'country will not be insulted' by the presence of the leading Nazi and founder of the Gestapo, Hermann Goering, at the forthcoming coronation of George VI.[32]

As she spoke, the clouds of war were gathering and Ellen would soon have to readjust her politics to suit the new challenges facing her and the country.

7

The Second World War,
1939–45

It was a typically frightful night in London. Buildings were burning, roads were blocked with rubble, broken glass lay on the pavements, water was gushing out from burst pipes and gas was escaping from the mains. Bomb craters were everywhere. People wandered around dazed: some held bundles of belongings rescued from their homes; others searched for lost loved ones in the ruins, hoping that there were no unexploded bombs about to go off. On such a night, when it was too dangerous for Parliament to sit after dark, and when bombs were falling on London with more than ordinary intensity, Ellen was driving around in the blackout, without any headlights 'cheering the people in the shelters, moving about all over the place from the church crypts to the pubs'. And sinking a pint with fire-fighters during a break in the bombing.

Britain was now at war with Germany. At her union conference Ellen told delegates that 'if ever there was a war that trade unionists could stand for with a straight eye and clear heart, it is this. We are standing up and demanding an end of this tyranny of Fascism.'[1] For once, Ellen was in step with the mainstream of the Labour Party. The war brought her a new crusade: British democracy itself, not just women, not just the working class, needed to be saved. The *Daily Herald* commented that Ellen discovered in herself a 'new dignity, a new calm assurance and a new indefatigable attention to duty'. Never a clinically detached observer, she would bring the same ardent commitment to fighting the war as she had to her previous struggles. At first, Ellen's status as a compassionate radical politician was confirmed. Later, as the war became more challenging and she abandoned many of the principles she once held inviolate, her reputation as a fiery socialist diminished.

Ellen had loathed Chamberlain's politics of appeasement. She thought he had prevaricated when Germany invaded Poland and had only reluctantly caved in to Parliamentary pressure and declared war. At the beginning, the war went badly and Ellen blamed Chamberlain for it. She considered his halting excuses about the failure of the war almost too painful to listen to and commented that 'like witnesses at a prolonged execution MPs have to sit through each stage as the Hero of Munich is dragged through humiliation after humiliation, his dry lips growing greyer with each new tale of woe'.

She thought Chamberlain should resign and in true conspiratorial fashion joined those who plotted his downfall. A stratagem to unseat Chamberlain was hatched in the NEC. Everyone on the Executive, not just Ellen, agreed that a 'drastic reconstruction of the Government' was vital and urgent in order to win the war.[2] On 7 and 8 May 1940, a debate took place in Parliament on the general conduct of the war and Chamberlain was put under intense pressure to quit. On 9 March an article by Ellen appeared in *Tribune* with the headline 'Will the Old Man Cling to Power?' In it, she argued that the war was a gloves-off fight with fascism with a Britain weakened by catastrophically bad leadership. Labour, she said, was resolute and would 'not enter any Government of which Neville Chamberlain is the head'. Her article, along with others in a similar vein, unleashed a wave of criticism of the Prime Minister. On 10 May Clement Attlee telephoned Chamberlain to tell him that the Labour Party would join the government – but only under a new Prime Minister.

Later that same day, Winston Churchill became Prime Minister. Ellen was delighted: 'the demands of Labour for a planned, all-out national effort were at last satisfied ... the Labour leaders entered a Coalition pledged to place the needs of the nation above sectional interests'.[3] Churchill's appointment gave Labour an opportunity for increased influence. He invited Clement Attlee to select Labour MPs for Government posts and Attlee chose a balance between bourgeois and working-class MPs. Churchill was very keen on Ellen Wilkinson. He proudly told his friends that he had formed the most broad-based Government extending from the extreme right-wing Lord Lloyd to

Ellen Wilkinson on the left. She returned the compliment saying that when she was interviewed for the post she 'felt that I had been in the presence of a very great man and a very great leader'. It was extraordinary that this former suffragist revolutionary could express such willingness to be employed by a Tory well-known for his repressive role in crushing suffragette demonstrations, rebellions and strikes in the United Kingdom. In answer to her critics she replied: 'We are fighting for our very lives.' Churchill, she believed, was the man for the hour: 'the ranks of labour have no cause to love him (but) he has been consistently anti-Nazi.'

Figure 7.1   Ellen at home. (Picture Post/Getty Images)

Churchill appointed Ellen to a minor Ministerial post in charge of hardship tribunals, a job she said that was 'after her own heart'. In October 1940 she was moved to work as joint Parliamentary Private Secretary to Herbert Morrison, who had himself just been promoted to Home Secretary. She shared the job with John Jagger. Ellen proved to be a loyal, hard-working and able Private Secretary. At first she was given special responsibility for air raid shelters and the care of the homeless, a job that fitted her compassionate personality and her practical and problem-solving approach.

Ellen Wilkinson, John Jagger and Herbert Morrison faced colossal challenges as the British civilian population came under attack. In London, a series of heavy bombings – the Blitz – began on Saturday 7 September 1940 and continued until May 1941, leaving 20,000 dead and approximately 70,000 wounded. In other places too the bombardment was horrific: 15 other cities, from Plymouth to Glasgow, suffered major raids. It is widely accepted that the bombing had a dreadful impact on public morale as those who survived frequently lost their family, their homes, their possessions and their courage. There was often no gas, no electricity, no water and no transport.

Ellen vowed to do as much as she could do to keep the population safe and public morale positive but it was a tough undertaking. Part of her new job was 'to put to bed each night, outside their own homes, 1 million Londoners'. On the first evening of her new appointment she visited the East End, talked to people about their experiences and listened. According to Ellen, five-sixths of her time was spent visiting shelters: in the earliest months of her job she spent nearly every night inspecting a shelter, speaking to people and taking notes on how to improve the enforced communal life. The *Daily Express* commented that 'going round with Ellen Wilkinson there were two things I liked about her, things that give me confidence in her approach to the problem – her energy and her natural touch with these people. She talked to the wardens and would always stop to talk to some man or woman and find their points of view.'[4]

Shelter provision was woefully inadequate when Ellen took over. Many upper class families fled to their country houses, others took refuge in the safe basements of their expensive clubs and partied the night away. The government requisitioned an unused tube station at Down Street for itself and equipped it with bathrooms and other conveniences. Ellen, making a point of her solidarity with the poor and the politically insignificant, declined to use it. Simple corrugated steel Anderson shelters had been erected in gardens and a number of civic shelters were built in large towns but these were not sufficient. The shelters were badly built and were very damp. It certainly appeared as if no one in authority was concerned about the lives of the many thousands who were poor and without influence.

Before she had been in office for a week Ellen put forward a scheme to improve shelter provision. She organised the delivery of new ones, soon called Morrison shelters, which would withstand bombs better. Ellen claimed that the 'ordinary reasonably well-built house afforded much more protection than was expected' and a booklet, *Shelter at Home*, was issued to show how people could turn their homes into 'an air-raid shelter giving a high degree of protection'.[5]

At the beginning of the bombing, Ellen encouraged people to stay in these home shelters or use small surface shelters. However once heavy bombing began, people wanted somewhere safer and quieter to sleep at night. Large numbers of people queued all day to enter 'Nightmare Arches', the shelter off the Commercial Road in the East End. More than 15,000 people slept there each night and the floor was soon covered with urine and excrement. Ellen began her job by making a tour. 'There is new hope', said the *News Chronicle* on Ellen's new appointment, 'for the thousands of shelterers in Nightmare Arches'.

Londoners, fed up with the inadequacy of official provision, used their own initiative. Many piled into the underground stations, looking for protection from the incessant bombing. By the end of September 1940 nearly 200,000 people were sleeping in 'the Tube'. Initially Ellen and the Government discouraged people from sheltering in the underground because they feared that such a troglodyte existence would lead to a 'peculiar mentality of resignation' and thus compromise the war effort. The government instructed London Transport to ban people from using the underground as accommodation but was forced to reverse its decision when large numbers of people ignored these rules and made the underground their nightly home. Ellen was also anxious that people 'were inviting tragedy' by grouping together in such large numbers.[6] In one incident on the Metropolitan line, 61 died and 220 were injured when a bomb fell directly on the station. Some challenged government provision in other ways. In September 1940 a group of people from Stepney burst into the Savoy Hotel and occupied the basement reserved for wealthy guests. Ellen's reaction was to requisition 500 private cellars for Londoners to shelter in.

In the early days of the war Ellen needed urgently to improve the conditions of communal shelters and London Underground stations. As usual, she threw herself into the challenge. She promised people, 'Safety, Sanitation and Sleep', a typical Ellen sound-bite highlighting people's understandable human urge for all three. She chivvied and bullied, encouraged and threatened, ordered and charmed. On one visit to Manchester, after Ellen had condemned the corporation for its damp, unhygienic and uncomfortable shelters they quickly built new ones, renovated the old ones and provided bunk-beds, canteens and sanitation for their inhabitants. By the spring of 1941, thanks partly to the efforts of Ellen, Londoners were sheltering underground in some relative comfort. Ticket systems of entry were established, over 200,000 bunks were installed and allocated to regular users of the shelters, canteen facilities were set up, chemical lavatories, ventilation, lighting and running water were provided. And in some shelters night classes, films and other activities were made available.

Despite these shelter improvements, people still got hurt and many were killed. Ellen, who had always taken her responsibility seriously, drove herself around to inspect air-raid shelters immediately after they had been bombed. Soon she was dubbed the 'Shelter Queen'. One newspaper commented that 'Miss Ellen Wilkinson's personal visits to the East End ... have done more to put heart and courage into East End families than anything that has gone before ... they needed badly what Miss Wilkinson is giving them – womanly sympathy carried further than mere words.'[7] People knew that Ellen's sympathy was real: her own home was bombed in November 1940 and when she was given alternative accommodation that too was bombed.

On 14 November 1940, 515 German bombers attacked Coventry. The city centre was laid waste: the magnificent cathedral destroyed, the medieval streets ruined, one-third of factories irretrievably damaged and 4,000 homes flattened. Hundreds of people were killed and hundreds more seriously injured. Herbert Morrison and the king went to visit: Ellen was not considered important enough. Nearly a year later, however, Ellen was asked to visit Coventry to inspect its shelter provision. On her visit, she found that Anderson shelters had not been erected because of a lack of materials, surface shelters were falling down because they had been shoddily built and large areas of the city were without shelter. At night there were only 2,352 bunks for 150,000 people. Ellen blamed the Coventry National Emergency Committee, hinting that the 'municipality has been talking too much and acting too little'.[8] She accused the committee of not using the money allocated by the government for shelter provision, for not requesting enough Anderson shelters and for being 'slow off the mark' in organising shelters. 'Coventry has received many compliments for the heroism of its people, every one of them deserved,' Ellen said, 'but the fact must not be used to cover up its own Council's slackness in providing shelters and the bad quality of much of what it did provide.'[9]

Regardless of the blackout and the dangers involved in any kind of travel, Ellen visited most regional cities. In Plymouth, after the dreadful bombing that destroyed much of the city, she stayed overnight with Nancy Astor and went with her to inspect the damage. She often visited Liverpool, probably the most heavily bombed city outside London. Between 1 and 2 May 1941, 680 bombers dropped 870 tonnes of bombs and over 112,000 fire bombs over the city. During this period half of Liverpool docks were put out of action, over 700 water mains fractured, gas and electricity was severely damaged and 500 roads closed to traffic. On the night of 3–4 May the fire brigade put out 400 fires. On one of her visits to Liverpool, Ellen advised women and children to get out of the vulnerable areas as public shelters were not an appropriate place for them to be. 'The more I see', she insisted, 'of shelters in bombed areas the more convinced I am that the policy of dispersal is the right one … Many underground shelters only give an illusory security'. Such experiences confirmed Ellen's belief that she was fighting a just war. She stated that 'I never realised what a vindictive person I was until I went through these cities'.

As Parliamentary Private Secretary, Ellen was caught in a vortex of ministerial discipline and her natural temperament. She was required to defend government policy and keep quiet on matters of national security, a difficult task for someone so outspoken. She often represented Herbert Morrison in the House of Commons: in 1942 alone Ellen responded authoritatively and unemotionally to a range of queries about shelter provision, fire prevention, and the national fire service. She was severely tested over the Bethnal Green disaster. On 3 March 1943 crowds at Bethnal Green Tube station 'got out of hand and frantic with nervousness, confusion and worry' about the heavy gunfire and bombing outside, rushed in to the station. Someone slipped.[10] In a few seconds people were crushed to death as more and more attempted to gain entrance. In all, 173 people, including 84 women and 62 small children, died. A full enquiry, held in secret, exonerated the local authorities and concluded that the disaster was caused by people losing their 'self-control' and causing the deaths and injuries. When asked in the House of Commons whether the enquiry into the disaster would be circulated to MPs, Ellen had to prevaricate. The enquiry was never published. Instead Morrison made a short statement in the House of Commons, and because of the risk to national security, made no reference to the panic of those involved. This generated resentment and the government was blamed for hushing up the disaster because of its own inadequacies. Ellen remained silent. Her ex-colleague, Wright Robinson, noticed a marked change in her behaviour. On a previous meeting she had 'criticised rather drastically and hastily our Air Raid Shelters. She had had less experience of responsibility. Now she has had more and finds that rip and run raids of freelances do not apply to ministers in office … I admire her for facing up to responsibility and taking the raps that come to people who do.'[11]

In January 1943 Ellen's empathy was tested to the limit when she visited Catford Central School, Sandhurst Road, in southeast London. Here 32 children and four teachers had been killed in a lunchtime air-raid. Ellen met as many bereaved parents as she could and tried to console them.[12] Where did she find the words to comfort Mr and Mrs Scholl, whose eleven-year-old daughter had been killed? Or to the parents of five-year-old twins Ann and Judith Biddle who were eating their school lunch when the school was bombed? Ellen was well known for her compassion but this was a dreadful challenge.

After May 1941, as Germany re-directed its attention to Russia, heavy and destructive raids were sporadic. Ellen breathed a sigh of relief. However, in June 1944 a new threat emerged: the V1s, known as flying bombs. For three months over 5,000 bombs hit Britain. Towards the end of July 1944 one flying bomb wrecked a store and a bus full of passengers had its top blown off. It was difficult to find an appropriate warning system without bringing the country to a halt so

Herbert Morrison and Ellen Wilkinson were instructed to reduce the amount of notice given to the population. Did she replace her natural compassion with political expediency?

The Fire Services

In April 1941, Herbert Morrison restructured the fire services. Ellen was asked to help and her new role demanded that she quell any protest from fire-men. Did this mark a shift to the right? Ellen naturally would have justified her behaviour by pointing out that Britain was at war and that national interests must override sectional ones. At the beginning of the war Britain's fire services were made up of professionals and volunteers, largely under the control of local authorities. The service was not efficient enough to respond swiftly to fire outbreaks so Morrison merged them and put them under the control of a new Fire Service Council. At the end of May, 1,400 local fire brigades were forced to amalgamate down to 32. Ellen was on the council and her job was to convince firemen to accept the changes. The *Tamworth Herald* thought her 'the most tactless woman who ever

Figure 7.2   Meeting the fire-guards. (People's History Museum, Manchester)

held minor office (and) staggered eight million fire guards when she remarked petulantly that the new regulations are not meant to be understood by them – all they had to do is just do what they are told'.[13]

On New Year's Day 1941 Morrison established compulsory fire-watching and put Ellen Wilkinson in charge of it. It was called the people's fire-army, but the people did not like it. Trade unions insisted that fire-watchers be paid for their time and accused the government of violating the wartime consultation process. Ellen tried to convince unions that voluntary fire-watching was for the common good but they replied: 'Why should I watch the boss's property?' Ellen, who in the past might have led the protest, was forced to endorse the Government's position: the needs of the country she now believed, were more important than the rights of the working class.

Ellen and John Jagger found themselves in conflict with their own union when they put forward their new policy. In the end Herbert Morrison was forced to pay a surprise visit to the NUDAW conference to rally support for them both. He was partially persuasive. The union agreed to fire-watch houses and municipal buildings but refused to protect business properties. NUDAW also insisted on equitable rotas, adequate rest, suitable rest rooms, beds and bedding, facilities for refreshment, protective clothing and fire-fighting equipment, travelling expenses and financial compensation if injured.[14]

Wilkinson, Morrison and Jagger even found it difficult to convince their Labour Party colleagues and other MPs to fire-watch. In February 1941 members of staff at Labour Party headquarters, Transport House only agreed to fire-watch after being threatened with dismissal. And the Houses of Parliament – which was hit by bombs 14 times during the war – suffered extensive damage because MPs were either too reluctant or too busy to do their duty.[15]

A serious shortage of fire-watchers remained in spite of government pleas and diktats so in August 1942 fire-watching was made compulsory for women. Public reaction was overwhelmingly negative. Very many women claimed exemption: in Coventry 25,000 out of the 37,500 women registered excused themselves from fire-watching.[16] And very many women failed to register at all. Ellen, who had recently fractured her skull in a car accident, was in charge of converting the public to these new measures. In spite of the considerable pain of her fracture and severe bruising, she carried on until her doctor insisted that she stay in bed for a week. It was a demanding task even for a healthy person, particularly when she drew criticism from the people who had once been her strongest advocates. At one Liverpool meeting in October 1942 Ellen faced an angry audience of nearly 2,000 people who opposed the new government measures. Once or twice it got nearly out of hand as people screamed at her. Ellen, however, 'managed it with great humour and characteristic adroitness'[17] and succeeded in getting her points across. One month later, she had another 'somewhat stormy passage' when she spoke to a boisterous audience of 1,500 at the Coventry Hippodrome. The meeting was frequently in a 'state of uproar, interruptions, cheers, and questions' and she was jeered when she claimed that the government had done a lot for Coventry.[18] Ellen insisted that she was not 'asking women to do what she did not do herself. I was out in the blitzes, every one of the nights. I have been a voluntary Fire Guard ever since there were voluntary Fire Guards and the place I watch is in the centre of London.'[19] And when women complained about their domestic and shopping difficulties if they were on duty as fire-fighters, she advised them to get their husbands to help more instead of going to the pub.[20] Ellen pretended to be unperturbed by the disturbances commenting that 'I love a meeting of this sort; it is so democratic'.[21]

At the 1943 NUDAW conference delegates objected 'to the compulsory fire-watching order for women, and particularly condemns the part played by Miss Ellen Wilkinson'. A heated debate took place and a couple of delegates made personal attacks on her. One delegate defended her by saying that to 'single out one of our colleagues who has done yeoman service to our Movement is mean and despicable.' Ellen, however, was capable of defending herself. Nearly all protests, she insisted, 'and I say that as a trade unionist and as a feminist', came from men's organisations.[22] Criticisms, one paper commented, would not cause Ellen any sleepless nights since she was used to it. Moreover, though condemned by former allies, she drew support from a new group of colleagues, none more so than Herbert Morrison.

Ellen was fully committed to the government and castigated those who criticised it. 'Back our men in Government', she pleaded with *Tribune*. 'Power', she told the NUDAW conference, 'means responsibility'. By now, she had jettisoned her belief in trade unions as a force for radical change. Trade unions, she claimed, 'could not get a big social programme and a radical and permanent change by industrial action alone'.[23] Ellen told conference delegates that to win political power and to hold it long enough and powerfully enough to make a real socialist change the Labour Party would have to appeal to the growing section of the middle of the road voter. It was a statement that Herbert Morrison might have made.

In the First World War Ellen had engineered a number of strikes and had been critical of a government which curtailed freedom. Now she supported wartime limitations. The Emergency Powers Act and Defence Regulations provided the government with powers to direct and control labour. Strikes and lock-outs were banned. Oppressive measures such as these would once have provoked a response from Ellen but now, as a member of government, she supported them. In August 1941, a dispute involving 2,000 skilled men in the northeast was settled when she persuaded the men to resume work.[24] 'If you want a fight,' she told them, 'fight Hitler'.

More compromise, and more criticism, followed. In January 1941, the viscerally anti-communist Herbert Morrison banned the Communist Party's newspaper, the *Daily Worker*, after a number of inflammatory articles in the paper had called for 'revolutionary defeatism'. In the past Ellen had protested against the curbing of free speech but now, faced with the situation of war and her position in government, she retracted her views, justified the ban and accused the *Daily Worker* of undermining the war effort. Ellen was forced to defend her new perspective to delegates at the NUDAW conference. She contended that the ban of the *Daily Worker* was a Cabinet decision and appealed to those in her audience who did not want to see these 'relations bedevilled by a group of irresponsible people running irresponsible campaigns at the most embarrassing time'.[25]

In June 1941, Hitler invaded Soviet Russia and Russia entered the war on the Allied side. As a consequence British communists once more regarded the war as a fight against fascism. By this time Ellen, exasperated by the irresponsible and unstable character of the British communists, had given up being friendly with them. When Ellen was asked about this she replied. 'I not only worked with the Communists but I risked my political career because of them' but now their policies appalled her. The communists, in turn, hated Ellen, possibly because she knew too much about them.[26]

Tensions between Ellen and trade unionists intensified. In October 1942, Ellen condemned workers at a shipyard in Newcastle upon Tyne who had gone on an unofficial strike. She hoped, she said, that they would lose. The government, keen to squash industrial action, also prosecuted 1,000 of 4,000 striking miners at a Kent colliery and imprisoned its main leaders. Eventually the case was dropped but such incidents led to further criticisms of her. At the 1943 NUDAW conference one delegate accused 'their' MPs of colluding in the repression of the working class, remarking that 'you cannot convert a prison van into a Rolls Royce merely by putting Ellen Wilkinson at the wheel'.

Ellen was now part of the political establishment and she reaped the rewards. In June 1941 the NEC suggested that she put her name forward for Vice-Chair of the NEC. Ellen declined, intimating that her duties as Parliamentary Secretary were so exacting that she did not desire nomination. In April 1943, she changed her mind, informed Hugh Dalton that she wanted to be Vice-Chair of the Party, and pointed out that on seniority grounds she was entitled to this. In June 1943 Ellen was duly elected Vice-Chair of the National Executive. In this post she was now an ex-officio member of all the sub committees but her preference was the election, the policy, and the organisation committees. In January 1945, when the Chair of the NEC died suddenly, Ellen became Chair and Harold Laski, Vice-Chair, of the Labour Party. Nevertheless, her previous reputation as a militant firebrand remained. One MP wrote in his diary 'if the Labour Party can survive these two appointments, it must be indestructible'; Hugh Dalton called them 'deplorably ill-timed' appointments. Ellen was still considered to be too much of a loose cannon with argumentative and contentious views which usually attracted trouble. Nonetheless, Ellen's rise in the political echelon was unstoppable. In January 1945 she was made Privy Councillor in the New Year's Honours List, and she was formally titled the Right Honourable Ellen Wilkinson MA.

By now Ellen's health was deteriorating rapidly. On 26 April she entered a nursing home and did not return to the NEC until June 1944. In November she was back in hospital and could not take the Chair at the December 1944 conference: she did not return until February 1945. By now Ellen had mellowed but she claimed that she had not changed her fundamental views. When an old comrade asked her 'Are you still uncompromisingly a Socialist?' she gave him a straight look and said with remarkable intensity 'Much more so than ever'. As a Right Honourable and a Parliamentary Secretary she had to exercise restraint but at times was unable to resist the temptation to shock the more conservative civil servants.[27] Certainly Ellen's public comments remained as radical as ever. On 24 March she confided to *Reynolds News* that she was worried that removals of economic controls post-war would lead to a 'hangover which would make the between wars depression seem like a Christmas party'. She feared that fortunes would be made by the 'worst kinds of speculators' if the Tory Party gained power. The election, she maintained, would be fought over whether the national needs would be met 'by the ethics of the poker table or by trained and intentional planning'. She accused the Tory Party of wanting to give employers all power in industry and the bankers all power in finance. Ellen also hit out at doctors and others who sought to undermine the National Health proposals: no sectional interest, she insisted, should be allowed to stand in the way of progress.[28]

Meanwhile, on 11 April 1945, Ellen Wilkinson accompanied Clement Attlee, Anthony Eden and Lord Halifax on an official visit to San Francisco to help set up the United Nations. Before they left they had a 'full and frank discussion'[29] with the NEC so that they could make decisions at the Conference which reflected Labour Party policy. It was their first experience of a major international diplomatic conference. The task of the delegates was to create a world organisation to replace the now defunct, and discredited, League of Nations. During the conference the war in Europe ended and the group returned to England. Soon Ellen and the Labour Party would need to find new energy for a long-delayed election campaign.

8

Post-war, 1945–47

On 30 April 1945 Hitler committed suicide. A few days later Germany surrendered and the war officially ended in Europe. No more bombs would be dropped, no more houses destroyed, no more families made homeless, no more people killed or injured and no more need for shelters or fire-watchers. Ellen collapsed in a relief-fuelled exhaustion. But she was left with no time to recuperate. On 23 May the Coalition government was replaced by a Conservative 'Caretaker' government; on 28 May Churchill hosted a farewell cocktail party at which Ellen, along with others, said their goodbyes; on 15 June Parliament was dissolved. On 5 July new elections took place.

During the war Ellen had held enormous responsibility for the lives of people. This, according to the *Daily Herald*, had added 'dignity to her wit'. She was now considered a 'cool woman, quietly but dapperly dressed ... an occasional spark in the frank eyes, hints that somewhere inside the young student who used to argue hotly about Votes for Women is still alive and giggling'. She continued to produce her familiar trenchant witticisms, once commenting that the House of Commons was a 'place full of ex-future Prime Ministers'. More importantly, she still believed in state control of the 'commanding heights' of the economy, but sought a parliamentary road to it, rather than a revolutionary one.

By now, Ellen was a key figure in the Labour Party and a senior member of the NEC. She was a member of the Policy Sub-Committee, the policy-forming body responsible for developing the economic and social agenda for the 1945 Labour government. She took part in all the key discussions. At the time the NEC supervised policy development and Ellen played a pivotal role, helping to direct policy and arguing for Labour to be more radical. The committee stressed that 'the ultimate aim of the Movement was socialism, which we believe can only be attained on the basis of democracy'.[1]

In April 1945, the National Executive Committee of the Labour Party, printed 100,000 copies of *Let us Face the Future*, a document which embodied years of work by the NEC.[2] Ellen co-authored the manifesto with Michael Young, Herbert Morrison and Patrick Gordon Walker.[3] Who wrote each section is difficult to ascertain, as it was promoted as a collaborative effort, but *Let us Face the Future* was a passionate, expressive, radical manifesto which had Ellen's hand, and principles, written all over it. The manifesto reminded readers that the Conservatives had handled the pre-war Depression badly as 'Big Interests had things all their own way'. And in a wonderfully apposite parody of Churchill's famous aphorism stated that 'Never was so much injury done to so many by so few'. The manifesto declared that the 'Labour Party stands for freedom – for freedom of worship, freedom of speech, freedom of the Press ... But there are certain so-called freedoms that Labour will not tolerate: freedom to exploit other people; freedom to pay poor wages and to push up prices for selfish profit; freedom to deprive the people of the means of living full, happy, healthy lives.'[4]

The nation, the manifesto went on to say, needed a tremendous overhaul, 'a great programme of modernisation and re-equipment of its homes, its factories and machinery, its schools, its social services'. The Labour Party pledged itself to full employment. 'No more dole queues in order to let the Czars of Big Business remain kings in their own castles. The price of "economic freedom" for the few is too high if it is bought at the cost of idleness and misery for millions.' One can almost hear Ellen speaking when the manifesto stated it would raise the level of production as 'firstly ... over production is not the cause of depression and unemployment; it is under-consumption that is responsible ... Secondly, a high and constant purchasing power can be maintained through good wages, social services and insurance, and taxation ... thirdly planned investment in essential industries and on houses, schools, hospitals and civic centres.'

She had long believed that 'to nationalise the banks is to attack the very citadel of capitalist supremacy', so was delighted when the manifesto declared that the Bank of England must be brought under public ownership. And in the gloriously socialist Clause IV – in hardly the words of Herbert Morrison – the Manifesto stated 'The Labour Party is a Socialist Party, and proud of it. Its ultimate purpose at home is the establishment of the Socialist Commonwealth – free, democratic, efficient, progressive, public-spirited, its material resources organised in the service of the British People.' The transformation of society that Ellen had worked for all her life now seemed possible. Socialism, or at least a form of it, would be achieved the parliamentary way: Ellen's youthful aim to follow a revolutionary road to socialism was now well and truly relinquished.[5]

On 21 May 1945, at the 44th annual conference of the Labour Party held in Blackpool, Ellen presided over the largest Labour Party conference ever held. She was now at the pinnacle of her power, sitting centre stage on the conference platform. In her opening speech, she spoke of how people must decide 'whether Britain will put itself again under the rule of Big Business, or whether we will advance towards a society in which the whole resources of the country are efficiently used in the interests of the community.'[6] We want, she informed her audience, millions of houses, jobs for all, social security, educational opportunity for everyone and a real State Health service. The conference, under Ellen's guidance, went on to debate *Let us Face the Future*.

In her concluding speech Ellen reminded delegates that they were fighting the 'Party of the rich, the Party of the powerful, the Party of big business, the Party that controls the great industries, the cartels and very largely the Press. These are our enemies.'[7] She concluded by saying 'Fight, fight clean, fight hard, and come back with a solid majority for a Labour Government.' It was a rousing, socialist speech and a strong rebuttal to those who castigate Ellen for sliding to the right.

Her union, so critical of her in recent years, was proud of the fact that one of its officials should have presided and prouder still that 'she discharged that responsibility with such outstanding success'.[8] It was, claimed a colleague, Ellen's finest hour. 'No one will ever forget the nerve, the verve, the wit, the confidence and the joyful challenge with which she led the Conference from its brilliant opening to its triumphant close.'[9] She inspired the conference with her absolute confidence that Labour would win. Ellen herself said: 'This is the proudest moment of my life.'

As soon as the news of the coalition's end was known Ellen's conspiratorial tendencies were evident once more and she began 'some very maladroit and ill-timed propaganda' against Clement Attlee at the Labour Party conference.[10] In 1945 Herbert Morrison was one of the most popular figures in the Labour Party and Ellen hoped he would take over as party leader. The *Daily Express*, probably briefed by Ellen, reported that Morrison was the 'present idol of the delegates and the undoubted leader of the Party today'. Even so, Ellen Wilkinson's promotion of Morrison as Labour Party leader was unwise. It was highly unlikely that conference delegates would want to change their leader when they were in the middle of discussing a party manifesto and preparing for the next general election. But Ellen was probably in love with Morrison and could not see the inappropriateness of her intrigues. At the social evening at the end of the conference Ellen and Herbert Morrison danced the last waltz, 'canoodling in a rather obvious manner'. It was the first time that the two had shown any amorous feelings about each other in public and their inhibitions were most likely swept away by the euphoric conference atmosphere.

Shortly after the conference, on 4 June, Ellen continued her campaign to oust Attlee by writing an attack on him in the *Sunday Referee*, a scurrilous popular paper devoted to social gossip. Attlee, she reported, was a quiet London member who should be replaced by 'that superb political organiser', Morrison. She also wrote an anonymous and even more unguarded criticism of Attlee in *Time and Tide*, arguing once more that Morrison was Labour's 'biggest personal asset. He has great achievements to his credit. His work is known all over the country ... Mr Attlee does not command that authority.'

Hugh Dalton noted in his diary that a row was rumbling. Some people were 'going about swearing that they would have Ellen's head on a charger'. At the NEC meeting, the new Chair, her former ally Harold Laski, raised 'with regret' Ellen's article and rebuked her for expressing a lack of confidence in the Labour leader just before an election. Hugh Dalton noted that the discussion which followed was angry and confused. She was not popular with most of the men at the best of times, and on this occasion she had infuriated three sections, Greenwood's friends, the loyal Attleeans and a number of members who simply rallied to the side of a sick man. She did not make a very good defence and she did not counter-attack.[11]

A vote of 'severe condemnation' of Ellen was proposed but later withdrawn when it was realised that opinion was divided on the question. Instead, the NEC passed a vote of confidence in Clement Attlee. Ellen abstained.

Ellen went into the election with her gun full of socialist ammunition, firing round after round of bullets at the Tory party. She was part of a special Campaign Committee, including Clement Attlee and Herbert Morrison, which directed the election. She hectored, wrote and spoke to as many as she could, reminding each audience of the bitter period of 18 years of inter-war Tory rule. One of nine celebrity MPs who broadcast to the nation, Ellen hit out against the proposed de-regulation of price controls. If controls were taken off, she argued, it would be 'a polka to perdition' and the 'biggest gamblers' clean up in history,' just like the 'mad orgy of uncontrolled capitalism' after the First World War. The Conservatives talked about protecting nest eggs, she said, but it would be 'scrambled nest eggs' if they had their way.

The Labour Party won a sweeping victory, winning an overall majority of 146. Labour took 393 seats, the Conservatives 213 and the Liberals only 12. Twenty-one female Labour MPs were elected. For the first time in its history Ellen's party was in full power. The future, she believed, could now be faced. A sense of optimism prevailed: Michael Foot called it 'the blissful dawn of July 1945'. Hopes were very high that the Labour government would not only solve the problems of post-war reconstruction but would make life considerably better for the working class. Certainly large numbers of the electorate, who still remembered the privations of the Conservative-dominated Depression years, passed a vote of no confidence in the past, and showed their preference for a British-style socialist revolution.

Ellen was returned to Parliament with a greatly increased majority of 11,007. On 11 October 1945 the London Co-operative Branch threw a victory party for the NUDAW-sponsored MPs. The hall echoed to the

noise of such an excited, happy throng as that which waltzed, fox-trotted and jittered … over 1,200 people twirled and whirled, danced and sang in expression of their warm welcome to the NUDAW contingent to the first Labour Government in power. As one watched well-known personalities as they threaded their way through the Conga-ing one had a complete realisation of the power and influence of the Union and of the great contribution it has made to the economic and social emancipation of the working class. Here was our Ellen, looking well and vigorous, enjoying an evening's respite.[12]

And yet even after the election Ellen continued to campaign for a leadership change. The night she returned to London to meet the new Parliamentary Labour Party, she urged recently elected Labour MPs to support a motion to elect Morrison. She tried to persuade Leah Manning at the meeting itself that Attlee must go saying: 'He's no good. We must have Herbert.'[13] Even in the lavatories, female MPs were not safe from her entreaties – she accosted Edith Summerskill in one and asked her to support Morrison for leadership.[14] Ellen's judgement had always had an emotional element and her love for Herbert Morrison was clouding her political judgement making her unable to see the absurdity of her proposals. Her hopes were irretrievably dashed when Attlee arrived at a Labour Party victory rally and was greeted with huge cheers of approval – he had already accepted the King's invitation to form a government. Morrison's chances of being the first among equals were scotched for the time being. Even so, Ellen remained resolutely committed to replacing Attlee – when the Prime Minister issued his first list of appointments she was still agitating for Morrison.

She was loyal to Winston Churchill in a way she never was to Clement Attlee. When Churchill returned to the House of Commons after his humiliating defeat Ellen, the only one on her side of the

House to do so, gave her former chief a sympathetic cheer as he entered the Chamber. She once remarked to a Labour colleague that 'It's no use asking me about Winston, I'm prejudiced in his favour'.[15] It was a remark characteristic of a generous, yet flawed, personality.

Labour's First Majority Government

Ellen's chief contribution to the post-war Labour government was as its social conscience, helping it to transform Britain at a time of economic austerity. She was part of a government, which apart from Aneurin Bevan, Emanuel Shinwell, Stafford Cripps and herself, held firmly to the centre-ground of the Labour Party. Figures like Clement Attlee (Prime Minister), Herbert Morrison (Lord President), Ernest Bevin (Foreign Secretary) and Hugh Dalton (Chancellor) dominated. Despite these difficulties the Labour government held to its electoral promise of reform. It created the National Health Service, introduced a more comprehensive system of national insurance, nationalised the Bank of England and key industries like coal and iron, repealed anti-union laws and reformed the education system. Ellen's hopes for her country seemed to have materialised.

On 3 August 1945 Ellen Wilkinson became the first female Minister of Education, the second woman in Britain to become a Cabinet Minister and the only woman in a Cabinet of 20. Historians

Figure 8.1 The Labour Party Cabinet, 1945. (People's History Museum, Manchester)

have expressed astonishment that Attlee gave 'Red Ellen' such an important post, especially when she had tried to depose him as leader, but this underestimates both Attlee's management skills and Ellen's importance. Firstly, she was a senior member of the Labour Party, had been Chair of the National Executive Committee, had co-written the manifesto, had proven her worth during the war, and was well known and popular. It would have been inconceivable for the Prime Minister to ignore her. Indeed, Attlee had first put Ellen down for Minister of Health but later crossed out her name and replaced it with Aneurin Bevan's.[16]

Secondly, Attlee wanted a woman in his Cabinet. Ellen had come a long way from her suffragist revolutionary past and was now the most important woman in the Labour Party.[17] Thirdly, Attlee shrewdly wanted a Cabinet balance of middle-class MPs and trade unionists and knew that Ellen represented both. She held a masters degree and was clearly one of the most able and articulate trade-union sponsored MPs. Fourthly, the principle of collective responsibility gave the Prime Minister an incentive to include political opponents in Cabinet in order to silence any criticism. Attlee was aware that the left was entitled to its share of Government and bringing in Ellen would appease, and hopefully restrain, them. Fifthly, Ellen was competent, having previously demonstrated the requisite skills of framing legislation and placing it on the statute books. Attlee knew that during the war she had placed the demands of government before principle or private belief and was now considered a safe pair of hands. Finally, and crucially, Attlee respected and liked her, having a huge regard for those like Ellen who had an inspiring vision of socialism and a visceral detestation of poverty.[18]

Yet Ellen was still reckless and indiscreet at times and her comments often generated controversy. In a characteristically off-the-cuff remark she told her Jarrow constituents that bread might be rationed if ships sent over to fetch grain did not reach Canada before the winter freeze. The Prime Minister was furious and Ellen was quickly recalled to London. Something needed to be done, the *Western Mail* urged, about the habit ministers had of making unauthorised pronouncements that seem to be unannounced Cabinet decisions. The doctrine of collective responsibility, it advised, needed brushing up. When Ellen was questioned in Parliament about her statements a great crowd of MPs assembled in the Commons to hear her and the mood was jovial. MPs of all parties entertained each other with caustic jibes before giving Ellen a rousing cheer and settling back to enjoy the prospect of her familiar ripostes. They were disappointed: her speech was not humorous at all. Instead Ellen, in a very serious manner, took the full blame for her misdemeanour and promised to be careful in future. Ellen, as Cabinet minister, could no longer afford to be entertainment fodder for the House of Commons.

Many feared, and some hoped, that Ellen's instinctive radicalism might collide with her ministerial brief. She was certainly still in contact with old communist friends: in March 1946 she wrote asking Morgan Phillips, the General Secretary of the Labour Party, for 'a special favour'[19] and give help to Otto Katz, known to British intelligence as a Soviet agent. However, as she grew older, and some say, grew up, Ellen developed into a fully rounded politician at ease with her ministerial status and for the short time she held the post worked comfortably within the strict parameters of her new job. Certainly she faced challenges not only as the first female Minister of Education but also as a feminist and socialist within a centre-left Cabinet. Even so, Ellen's contribution to the post-war government more generally was perhaps not as great as she hoped, partly because of her chronic asthma and lung problems and partly because her new job commanded so much of her time.

As a Cabinet minister, Ellen was responsible for the work of her department, was its spokeswoman in Parliament, and represented it to the outside world. Her main task as a minister was to implement the Conservative MPs' 'Rab' Butler's 1944 Education Act which set out a controversial tripartite system of grammar schools for the most intellectually gifted, modern schools for the majority and technical schools for those with a technical or scientific aptitude. To assess who should attend which state school, pupils took an exam when they were eleven years old, known as the eleven plus. Those who passed went to the grammar schools whereas those who failed went to secondary moderns.

It was set to be Ellen Wilkinson's last big challenge. In her own lifetime, educational Acts, such as the Fisher Act, had been passed but not put into effect either through a lack of will or a change of government. Colleagues congratulated Ellen on her boldness and decisiveness since the 'Act looked as though it were drifting into the doldrums'.[20] Some historians seem to think that her appointment was unfortunate because the previous neglect of education required someone with exemplary administrative skills and an ameliorative way with officials, qualities apparently missing in Ellen Wilkinson. This is a misjudgement: she had proven administrative skills and a persuasive personality. Regrettably, she was required to enact an Education Act she had not written. *The Tribune* believed that 'we do not doubt that she will strive to instil into it the maximum socialist content, but it is not the Act which she would have fashioned if she could have started afresh'.

Many thought it would be impossible to introduce any measure of educational reform at a time of economic constraint and Ellen complained to Harold Laski that she had 'a hell of a job here because of the shortage of everything and the difficulty of ever getting the Ministry of Works to do anything to time'.[21] Certainly Britain's severe post-war difficulties meant that it was hardly a propitious time for expansion. The country was on the verge of bankruptcy, had lost approximately one quarter of its wealth, lost many of its overseas assets and was dependent on the US for loans. Ellen had to persuade a reluctant Cabinet to provide the money for reform, chivvy the building industry and train the new teachers. 'But I never doubted', commented Susan Lawrence 'that in spite of all the frightful obstacles – want of teachers and want of buildings – that Ellen would find a way, and she did, where a weaker Minister might well have shrunk from all the lions in the path'.[22]

Ellen was motivated by her conviction that education was a force for social change and a way to increase social capital. Investment in people's education, she believed, was the key to economic, social and political advancement. When she went to the Ministry of Education, she said:

I had two guiding aims, and they come largely out of my own experience. I was born into a working-class home, and I had to fight my own way through to the University. The first of those

guiding principles was to see that no boy or girl is debarred by
lack of means from taking a course of education for which he or
she is qualified ... the second one was that we should remove
from education those class distinctions which are the negation
of democracy.[23]

Given her radical past, many hoped that Ellen would eradicate the
elitism central to the British educational system and rectify some of
the inequalities of Butler's Act. She did not. Using a booklet written
by the previous Conservative regime, *The Nation's Schools*, Ellen and
her team re-affirmed Labour's commitment to the Act. The left-wing
of the Labour Party were outraged, condemned the pamphlet as
class-ridden and profoundly reactionary and asked that the socialist
Minister of Education 'burn it'.[24] Jean Mann recalls 'that just after
receiving a barrage from the Labour benches, Ellen came down to
the Ladies Members' Room, shaking and upset. In the ruthless attack
on her there were no holds barred and no regard made for the fact
that Ellen was suffering from extreme physical disability.'[25] Ellen
withdrew the booklet but the policy remained.

Ellen had been educated at a grammar school and she had a strong
loyalty to the elitist system which had helped her succeed. She had
envisaged that there would be parity of esteem between the three
school systems but this hope never materialised as Technical schools
were expensive to manage and LEAs were reluctant to build them.
The education system imagined by Ellen was bipartite rather than
tripartite; and the bipartite system was deeply flawed. She appealed
to educationalists and teachers to guard against any tendency to
see secondary modern schools as dumping grounds for children
but her words went largely unheeded. Local Education Authorities
remained unwilling to build more grammar schools so there was
fierce competition for places. Only 20 per cent of school pupils
'passed' the eleven plus examination; the rest, who had 'failed', the
majority of working-class children, went to the secondary moderns.
The damage to the self-esteem of the eleven-year-olds who failed was
considerable.

Ellen drew support from the left-wing of the Labour Party when
she raised the school-leaving age from 14 to 15, persuaded Parliament

to pass the 1946 School Milk Act that gave free milk to British school children, reduced the number of direct-grant schools and instituted university scholarships to help towards the cost of higher education for those who could not afford to pay. Raising the school-leaving age was an ambitious task as the Blitz had destroyed a great many schools and teachers were in short supply. It required every ounce of determination Ellen could muster to do this. She had to find 5,000 extra classrooms and train 13,000 more teachers for the expected extra 390,000 pupils. The Labour Cabinet, hard-pressed by post-war financial limitations, was disinclined to allocate sufficient money. In several Cabinet meetings, and with Attlee's support, she fought against three heavyweights, and friends – Dalton, Cripps and Morrison – to gain the necessary funding for raising the school-leaving age. After a series of battles she eventually told the Cabinet that if it refused to back her she would campaign outside Parliament. 'As a trade union official', she insisted, 'I am quite fully prepared to use my union, public platforms and the press to argue the case'.[26] The Cabinet conceded.

As Minister of Education, she had to oversee a very large school-building programme. There was no money to build new schools or new extensions so the pragmatic Ellen devised special prefabricated huts to accommodate the new pupils. She defended these huts saying 'I know that some of these huts look very functional … but they generally are much cleaner, more sanitary and more weatherproof than many of the picturesque old buildings … They are not disused Army huts, they are proper huts, well designed for their job'.[27] The last remaining 'temporary' school hut was demolished in the Wirral in 2012.

Ellen had to overcome a shortage of teachers both because of the war and because of the raising of the school-leaving age. She set up a one-year Emergency Training Scheme: generous grants were given to ex-service men and women between the ages of 25 and 30 to train as teachers. They were housed in 'hastily improvised colleges which ranged from a Duke's castle in Northumberland to groups of munition works near Wednesbury'.[28] Labour MPs and others complained that the emergency training scheme would dump hordes of ill-trained teachers on the schools but Ellen took no notice.[29]

In a joint memorandum, Ellen and the Secretary of State for Scotland advocated free milk and free meals for children in primary and secondary schools.[30] Together, they reminded the Cabinet that before the war, when malnutrition was rampant, the Tories had refused to give milk and school meals to children because they said it undermined parental responsibility.[31] Their success in convincing the Cabinet to provide free milk was an important achievement. A number of working-class and poorer children did not eat adequately, were malnourished and often left home without breakfast. It is said that generations of children grew up stronger and healthier because of this measure. It more or less remained in force until Margaret Thatcher was ordered to abolish it by the Chancellor when she became Education Secretary in 1970.[32] Free school meals, although only for infants in primary schools, will be introduced in 2014.

The expansion and improvement of technical education was high on Ellen's list of priorities. In her view, a better technical education was needed for Britain's industrial reconstruction and the revival of the export trade. She aimed to promote new schemes in more than 20 industries including mining, building and the motor trade. Her policy operated on three levels: national, regional and local – buzzwords today but refreshingly new at the time. Ellen opened the College of Aeronautics at Cranfield which provided a residential two-year postgraduate course for 50 aeronautical science and engineering students. Money again was limited so instead of a brand new purpose built college the government converted the site of a former RAF base. The airmen's dining hall was divided up for a library, a lecture hall, two common rooms and a staff room, the barrack blocks were transformed into laboratories and the sergeants' mess into a hall of residence. The college eventually developed into a highly successful graduate centre for science, engineering, technology and management: Cranfield University.

As a committed anti-fascist, Ellen took an interest in what was happening in post-war Germany. In October 1945 Attlee asked her to visit Berlin and the British Zone in Germany to get a general sense of what was going on politically, and to review the educational facilities there. Attlee knew about Ellen's pre-war involvement in Germany, knew that she was respected in socialist circles and believed that she had the ability to see, comment upon and advise on its reconstruction.

In a secret, and long, memorandum Ellen outlined the problems and possibilities of rebuilding a post-war Germany. She used a measured, academic and neutral tone to describe conditions there. When Britain first overran Germany, she wrote, it was an 'administrative desert' with no industry, no communications, no electric power and no local government. Like most defeated countries there was a shortage of food, shortage of coal, shortage of manpower, shortage of accommodation and serious health issues. 'Typhus and typhoid', she noted were 'under control. Diptheria has been bad in some areas and so had tuberculosis, and venereal disease has been rampant.' Added to which there were, in the British zone alone, some 2.25 million displaced persons, 2.5 million German troops living in open fields and masses of refugees from the East entering the zone at a rate of some 9,000 a day. And as she stated in her report, life in post-war Germany was dangerous for a lot of people as 'there were naturally many cases of murder and rape, (even though) there were no attempts at massacre of the German population on any considerable scale'.[33]

At this point, Ellen was completely disillusioned with Soviet Russia. She condemned the Russians for 'not worrying very much about what happens to the Germans and in particular how many of them die or contract diseases during this winter ... Russians are stripping the zone which they occupy of as much material and plant as they can carry away to Russia'. She spoke of the difficulties of establishing democracy in Germany, especially when the Russians tried to undermine it. Ellen, as a former trade unionist and trade union sponsored MP, believed that trade unions, which had been abolished by the Nazis, could act as a powerful democratising force and welcomed the fact that they were being re-built slowly. Every factory election, she wrote, was a struggle between the two main left-wing parties for control of the unions but Ellen maintained that 'this struggle has to be fought out if German democracy is to be born ... These factory struggles may throw up much-needed new leadership'.[34]

However Ellen's main job was to report on the educational system, seen as an important tool for the reconstruction of democracy in Germany. She gave an incisive picture of educational facilities, or the lack of them, in the occupied country. Shortage of administrative staff, shortage of schools, shortage of appropriate teaching staff and shortage of textbooks were matters of some concern. Ellen was not directly responsible for education in Germany, this was the job of the Control Commission, but her thinking on the subject was welcomed. She saw the task as firstly to set up an efficient administration, secondly to open the schools in 'reasonably tolerable conditions' and thirdly to see that education was underpinned by democratic values. Ellen spoke of how teachers were vetted 'with some care', with a number dismissed for their Nazi activities.[35] There were, she noted, 'no real suitable textbooks in any subject – even introductory books for little children were sheer Nazi propaganda.'

Figure 8.2   Ellen chairing the first UNESCO conference. (© UNESCO)

In November 1945 Ellen chaired a conference which aimed to establish 'an educational and cultural organisation of the United Nations (UNECO). Delegates from 45 countries ranging from Argentina through to Yugoslavia attended, but no representative from the USSR was present. Ellen asked the Prime Minister, Clement Attlee, to welcome the delegates to the conference. He agreed to do so – as long as she wrote a draft of his speech.[36]

At the founding conference Ellen suggested that Science be included in the title of the organisation since

> in these days when we are all wondering, perhaps apprehensively, what the scientists will do to us next, it is important that they should be linked closely with the humanities and should feel that they have a responsibility to mankind for the result of their labours. I do not believe that any scientists will have survived the world catastrophe, who will still say that they are utterly uninterested in the social implications of their discoveries.

The delegates, all too aware that the dropping of atom bombs on Hiroshima and Nagasaki had made Science a very topical subject, agreed. And so the United Nations Educational, Scientific and Cultural Organisation (UNESCO) was born.

The conference split up into commissions to agree the terms of a Constitution. This had originally been drafted by 'Rab' Butler and had been developed by Ellen at several meetings. The final draft certainly mirrored Ellen's style:

> that since wars begin in the mind of men, it is in the minds of men that the defences of peace must be constructed; that the great and terrible war which has now ended was a war made possible by the denial of the democratic principles of the dignity, equality and mutual respect of men, and by the propagation ... of the doctrine of the inequality of men and races.

At the end of the conference UNESCO's ultimate goal was defined: it would contribute to 'peace and security by promoting collaboration among the nations through education, science and culture.' Once the conference was over the Commission began to put its strategies in place. The Commission, with representatives from 14 countries, was presided over by Ellen and on 4 November 1946 UNESCO was given official status as an agency of the United Nations. UNESCO's first official conference was held in Paris later that year: Ellen was extremely disappointed not to be there but she had been taken ill.

Indeed, Ellen's health was deteriorating fast. All her life she had suffered from asthma, bronchitis, influenza and lung infections. During the war she had been admitted to hospital at least seven times. Exhausted by the war effort her health was undermined further by the demands of her new post. She was plagued by serious illnesses aggravated by unremitting work, smoking and an exceptionally harsh winter. One of her last achievements was opening, with Laurence Olivier, the Old Vic Theatre School. The school building had been bombed and at the time of opening on 24 January still had no roof. Ellen caught pneumonia and a few weeks later, on 6 February 1947, she died in a private ward at St Mary's Hospital Paddington.

Conclusion

Many think that Ellen Wilkinson may have committed suicide and that the government hushed up the cause of her death because of the political embarrassment that would be caused by a senior figure taking her own life. But that seems improbable. There was an inquest: the coroner reported that Ellen died from heart failure as a result of emphysema, acute bronchitis and bronchial pneumonia, exacerbated by barbiturate poisoning. It was, he claimed, an accidental death.

Perhaps Ellen may have deliberately hastened her death by taking an overdose of barbiturates because, as she well knew, she did not have long to live. Serious bouts of pneumonia and very severe attacks of asthma had undermined what health she had left and she knew she was terminally ill. Ellen was also addicted to prescription drugs. In the 1940s asthma was seen as a psychosomatic illness and patients were treated for depression. Consequently she was prescribed drugs used to reduce mental and physical stress, rather than ones that might counter the effects of asthma. Sleeping pills were also prescribed for her asthma-induced insomnia. If her attack of asthma had been particularly acute and she was finding it hard to breathe, she may have taken a fatal dose of her prescribed drugs to ease the congestion. Or, knowing she was dying, may have wanted to control her death.

What is certain is that Ellen's ill-health, exacerbated by over-work, was a constant problem. Early in her career, the *Sunday Sun* commented that 'she lives on her nerves. She not only burns the candle at both ends but she tries to light it in the middle and she cannot bear the strain'. Her good friend Margaret Rhondda believed Ellen died of exhaustion. She had seen that Ellen's 'end must come fairly soon, but that she must have known it ... she has looked death in the face'.[1] It was common knowledge that Ellen had energy and a work ethic out of all proportion to her size and physical strength, and this inevitably resulted in her body giving up the struggle.

Ellen was buried in Penn Street near Amersham in Buckingham-shire. A simple stone engraved 'Ellen Wilkinson 1891–1947', marks her grave. Most of the great and good, with the exception of Herbert Morrison, attended her funeral. Morrison was gravely ill and in hospital at the time, recovering from an attack of thrombosis which had developed life-threatening complications. The BBC agreed to delay the news of Ellen's death until Herbert Morrison was told because his colleagues feared that it might kill him. When he heard, 'Morrison did not say anything, but suddenly looked years older'.[2] At the next NEC meeting her colleagues stood in silence.[3] Morrison, still seriously ill in hospital, was not present.

Ellen left all her property, worth £7,253, to her sister Anne Elizabeth but left no personal papers. They were destroyed. What was there to hide? Did she ever keep a diary? Were there incriminating letters from lovers? Were there notes from Herbert Morrison? Was there harmful information about her former Communist Party activities? Did she keep the names of revolutionaries she had once worked with? Were there any financial receipts from the Soviets? Were there records of her subversive actions in Germany and Spain? Was there any damaging evidence that might implicate others? Were there notes about illegal activities? So many questions to which there are no valid answers.

The obituaries point to Ellen's personality remaining relatively unchanged throughout her life. The *New York Times* could not 'forget the amazing amount of energy and passion, gaiety and vivaciousness compressed into 4ft 9". She was a strong-willed, empathetic, warm-hearted, generous woman who brought to 'public affairs an acute mind, an ebullient spirit and a passion for social justice, an intuitive and devoted partisanship for the poor and the weak'. Nonetheless, as with so many successful politicians, social reformers and political activists, she 'had a necessary vein of intransigence and could be 'an uncomfortable colleague as well as a ruthless opponent'.[4] Her rebellious nature, somewhat inhibited by high office, did not disappear. In his obituary, the communist leader Ian McKay wrote that she was a great fomenter of trouble, and wherever there was a row going on in support of some good – or even fairly good – cause that rebellious redhead was sure to be seen bobbing about in the heart of the tumult … and, if she mellowed a little towards the end … it only needed some cynical after-dinner gibe from one of the Tory diehards to rouse the old devil in her and show that behind the correct, austere façade of the Cabinet Minister there still pulsed the hot angry heart of the poor penniless but dauntless Lancashire lass who had fought her way up, past all the pomp and privileges, from the slums of Ardwick to the seats of the mighty.

If Ellen's political outlook shifted to the right as she got older it was probably because she was now in a position to get things done rather than point out what others ought to be doing. Undoubtedly Ellen had a multiple political individuality that escapes easy definition: she was a socialist, a feminist, a trade unionist, a pacifist, a Wesleyan Methodist, a vegetarian, an anti-fascist, an internationalist, a parliamentarian, and at one time, a revolutionary. Indubitably, there were tensions inherent in each stage of her journey as she balanced the sometimes competing ties of gender and class, of fostering peace yet fighting dictatorships, of Marxist theories and religious beliefs, of revolutionary politics and parliamentary democracy, of union solidarity and wartime exigencies, of nationalism and internationalism. It proved impossible for her to construct a coherent 'version' of her life, however principled she might want it to appear, without meeting difficulties and tensions. 'Red Ellen' remained throughout her life a socialist and feminist but these were negotiated terms, not fixed.

However, it is safe to say that the core of Ellen's character remained constant. She was warm, kind, loyal and exceedingly hard working. To the end she was likely to do something that was rash and impulsive. She was, after all, passionate rather than calm; emotional and warm rather than cool and distant; concerned and involved, rather than detached or objective; and sometimes wrong-headed and unfair. She judged with her heart rather than her head and tended to become angry and tearful at injustices. Throughout her short life, she was involved in so many of the important left-wing issues of the day. But she was no unthinking 'ism'-ist from the loony left, nor was she an 'infantile disorderly' revolutionary. Ellen wanted results and her politics became increasingly pragmatic. So many different groups of people had reason to be grateful for her contribution to transforming their lives: young women under 30 who benefited from equal franchise; women married to foreigners who retained their citizenship; female civil servants who campaigned for equal pay; women police officers for their existence; her Jarrow constituents for alleviating unemployment; trade unionists for improvements in union law; walkers who wanted the right to roam in the countryside;[5] borrowers who bought goods on hire purchase; wartime city dwellers for keeping them safe from bombs; Italian, Spanish and German socialists for her anti-fascist crusades; and Indian nationalists for publicising their cause. Everyone, save the bankers and other capitalists, had reason to thank Ellen for trying to safeguard their economic rights. In addition the post-war generation are indebted to her for helping to shape the Labour programme for social, economic and cultural change.

Reform or Revolutionary Change?

As England battles with a worsening economy, high unemployment and growing disaffection with parliamentary politics so Ellen Wilkinson's life is brought into sharper focus. Certainly she has deep resonance for anyone interested in politics today and particularly for political activists. Her passionate concern for the poor provides a much needed contribution to the economic debate especially as both the current Prime Minister, David Cameron, and Chancellor, George Osborne, seem to have no emotional understanding of the lives of those who are only managing to survive and insist on lowering already inadequate standards by their vicious cutbacks. As a back-bencher Ellen bombarded the inter-war Conservatives with impassioned attacks on their short-sightedness and self-interest and sought to undermine their reactionary programme. Her criticism of a government which ignored the needs of the most vulnerable, which advocated swingeing cuts at the expense of social justice, which ignored the northern industrialised counties in favour of the southern financial and banking services was uncannily pertinent in 2013. Present-day coalition rhetoric that the government wants to make Britain's economy better balanced, more dynamic and debt-free perfectly echoes the pronouncements of the Conservative-dominated National government of the 1930s. Ellen would have wanted to loosen restrictive fiscal policy and pump money into the economy; the bankers, she always believed, were more than capable of looking after themselves. However, Ellen Wilkinson was neither a profound nor an original economic thinker. The key lesson she teaches is not anything specific: it is the need for engagement, compassion, energy, concern and courage – freshened with a dash of utopian thinking.

But how best to put Ellen's socialism into practice? Her own methods of achieving her goals fluctuated. Out of Parliament, she advocated an uncompromising revolutionary socialism. 'What the younger generation is beginning to see', she wrote, 'and what the older leaders will never admit, is that reformism and Socialism are incompatible, that it is not in fact possible to get Socialism bit by bit ... A compromise between capitalism and Socialism is impossible.'[6] In her opinion, reformism split and isolated the working class by driving a wedge between the employed and unemployed, between town and country, between workers and the working middle-class, and between those who received state benefits and those who did not. In addition, she maintained, socialism was not a gift to be given to the nation by the Parliamentary Labour Party. Only a revolutionary socialist party, based on the active participation of the ordinary person, would be able to generate sufficient steam to change the world. Certainly, Ellen wanted to reach out to the ordinary person, not just the politically committed. She wrote books, including two political novels, and during her lifetime was one of the most widely-read female political journalists, often writing for the national daily press. Basically, she wanted socialism, and wanted as many people as possible to embrace it. To achieve this, Ellen targeted a mass audience and her accessible and engaging style ensured a wide readership for her ideologically motivated writing. She made even revolutionary socialism sound practical and attractive, and not frightening at all.

So is this a moment for the revolutionary change that Ellen Wilkinson once proposed?

Parallels certainly can be drawn. In the 1930s she witnessed an economic disaster: banks collapsed, businesses went bust, consumer spending plummeted and unemployment rose. The inter-war British Conservative-led Coalition government, and other European countries too, introduced austerity measures and cut public spending; Parliamentary democracy was challenged by both fascism and communism, both of which became terrifyingly viable. Democracy collapsed in parts of mainland Europe. Closer to our own time, the global financial crisis of the early twenty-first century is considered the worst since the 1930s, with today's deficit considerably worse than the debt of the previous catastrophe. Banks collapsed, businesses went bust, housing was devalued, consumer spending plummeted, currencies lost their status and unemployment rose. The government, keen to cut its deficit, introduced austerity measures: cuts in public spending led to increased poverty for society's most vulnerable, and wide-spread unrest in the inner cities of England. The lessons learned from the Depression were thought relevant; even the Prime Minister, David Cameron, talked about a crisis in capitalism. Bankers' greed, high unemployment, a disaffected youth without much hope, cynicism about government, the police and the press, riots in the street and schisms in the political elite pointed to an increasing desire for transformation. In 1939, largely because of the expansion of the arms industry, the rapid consumption of weapons, and a willingness of governments to accept budget deficit, Britain and the rest of the world climbed out of Depression. How will Europe and the rest of the world overcome their economic woes?

There is no agreement about what might take the place of capitalism today. Revolutionary socialism is not a plausible alternative given the experiences of it in Eastern Europe, Russia, China, Cuba and elsewhere. Stuart Hall, interviewed in February 2012, argued that 'the left is in trouble. It's not got any ideas. It's not got any independent analysis of its own, and therefore it's not got any vision'.[7] In its place, nationalism and/or religious fundamentalism are likely to dominate – certainly there is a dangerous move towards both in many parts of the world. At the time of writing, Hungary, under the leadership of Viktor Orban, seems to be creeping towards fascism: his government is increasingly authoritarian; press freedom is curtailed; people are dismissed from their jobs for being of the wrong political persuasion; the judiciary are under threat; and nationalism is rife. Rather alarmingly, certain mayors and local governments are eager to name their main square, Horthy Square, after the right-wing politician responsible for the deaths of communists in the 1930s. Indeed, there is an ideological push to reconstruct those times (anti-communist, non-democratic, implicitly anti-semitic) and re-instate the spirit and culture of those years.[8] Elsewhere, as in America, the Ukraine and Iran, right-wing anti-feminist and anti-gay religiosity threatens to undermine liberal and socialist philosophy.

Can there ever be a parliamentary road to socialism? When she was an MP, Ellen certainly thought so. She told her union journal that she did not

> want to seem too pessimistic about Parliament … For Parliament to do anything at all for the workers there must be a real majority of Labour – and that sustained over a good number of elections … Parliament has to be rescued from being the register of the rich man's will, the excellent club, the interesting debating society. It can be the mighty engine of the people's liberties if the people will use its levers and back their votes by great and powerful industrial organisation.[9]

By the outbreak of the Second World War she had spent long enough in the political wilderness of the far left, had witnessed the success of fascism and the collapse of her ideals in Soviet Russia to realise that the exercise of influence and power outside the democratic process was problematic. In the end, Ellen chose to work within the existing structure of political power, believing that parliamentary democracy was a more effective route for radical activists than criticising and organising from outside. Moreover, as she came to realise, the majority of people had no wish to change the system completely and merely wanted to tinker with the parts so that it became a little fairer. In her view, parliamentary democracy could offer a way forward if the

Labour Party would only decide to be more courageous. In post-war Britain it was and, whatever the criticisms of the first majority Labour government, it was a genuinely reforming government. Today, Ellen Wilkinson's words to the British Labour Party would undoubtedly be: 'Revive the spirit of '45!'

Notes

Preface

1. USDAW (Union of Shop, Distributive and Allied Workers) was formed in January 1947. It started life as the AUCE and in January 1921 became NUDAW.
2. Attlee correspondence and papers, 18 May–13 August 1945.
3. Ellen appears as Lysistrata in G.B. Shaw's, *The Apple Cart* and as the Headmistrress in Winifred Holtby's *South Riding*.
4. William Shakespeare, *A Midsummer Night's Dream*.
5. Susan Lawrence, *Fabian Quarterly*, March 1947.
6. *Daily Express*, 9 September 1931, p. 8.
7. Jonathan Dudley, September, 2010.

Chapter 1

1. Census return, 1891. Richard was employed by the National Mutual Philanthropic Collecting Society, based in Hyde.
2. This quote and other unattributed quotes come from newspaper collections located at the People's History Museum or the Modern Record Centre, University of Warwick. Space prohibits independent footnotes. Please contact me at paulabartley@outlook.com for the exact references.
3. Friedrich Engels, *The Condition of the Working-Class in England*, 1844.
4. Stella Davies, 'The Young Ellen Wilkinson', *Memoirs and Proceedings of the Manchester Literary and Philosophical Society*, 1964–65, p. 2.
5. This and much of the following information is from Ellen Wilkinson's chapter in *Myself When Young*, Frederick Muller, 1938, p. 402.
6. *Guardian*, 19 November 1941, p. 2.
7. Chris Wrigley, *Oxford Dictionary of National Biography*.
8. Letter to George Middleton, 13 July 1938.
9. *The New Dawn*, April 1923.
10. Minutes of the MSWS Executive Committee, 2 September 1913.
11. MSWS Annual Report, 1913.
12. Ellen was sent to help J.R. Clynes and others in the forthcoming election.
13. MSWS Annual Report, 1914.

14. *The Common Cause*, 10 October 1913, p. 469.
15. MSWS Executive Report, 31 March 1914.
16. *The Common Cause*, 14 August 1914, p. 391.
17. MSWS Executive Report, 6 October 1914.
18. *The Common Cause*, 20 November 1914, p. 554.
19. Ellen is listed as Honorary Secretary in the Women's Emergency Corps, Half Yearly Report, August 1914 to 31 January, 1915.
20. Women's Emergency Corps, Half Yearly Report, August 1914 to 31 January 1915; *The Gentlewoman*, 29 August 1914.
21. For example, the Duchess of Sunderland, the Marchioness of Londonderry. First Annual Report Women's Emergency Corps, 1914–15.
22. Letter to Middleton, undated but circa February 1915. Thank you Dr Alison Ronan for giving me a copy of this letter.

Chapter 2

1. AUCE Organising District Secretaries' Expenses, November 1918.
2. *The New Dawn*, 28 April 1923.
3. *Ibid.,* 2 September 1939, p. 548.
4. *The AUCE Journal*, September 1917.
5. *Ibid.*, July 1918, p. 3.
6. *The Co-operative Employee*, October 1916, p. 71.
7. *The New Dawn*, 22 July 1922, p. 9.
8. The Trades Board Act 1909 set up Boards to fix minimum rates of wages. Initially only four trades were included in the Act but this was later extended and in 1917 Ellen was largely responsible for setting up the Joint Laundry Board.
9. *The AUCE Journal*, March 1918, p. 190.
10. *Ibid.*, September 1916, p. 58.
11. AUCE leaflet, 16 September 1916.
12. AUCE Annual Report, 31 December 1917.
13. *The AUCE Journal*, May 1918, p. 81.
14. In 1915 a number of Craft Unions objected to skilled workers joining the AUCE (Amalgamated Union of Co-operative Employees) and had asked the Union to expel them.
15. AUCE letter to Branch Secretaries, October 1918.
16. Minutes of Executive Council Meeting, 15 December 1919.
17. General Secretary's Report, Sunday, 9 February 1919.
18. Minutes of Executive Council Special Meeting, London, 2 March 1919.

19. National Conference of Women, 15 and 16 October 1918, p. 99.
20. Minutes of General Purposes Committee SJCIWO, 8 February 1923.
21. Special Report on Staff Re-Organisation and Equipment, 5 June 1919.
22. *Labour Woman*, October 1924, p. 156.
23. *The New Dawn*, 7 January 1922, pp. 7–8.
24. Cave Committee Inquiry, 1922.
25. Wright Robinson, 1921, MRO.
26. *Ibid.*, 24 May 1923, p. 110.
27. *The New Dawn,* 7 July 1923, p. 8.
28. *Labour Woman,* 1 July 1923.
29. Annual Delegate Meeting, 9 April 1917.
30. John Callaghan, *Rajani Palme Dutt,* Lawrence & Wishart, 1993, p. 34.
31. Report on Revolutionary Organisations in the United Kingdom, 9 June 1921.
32. *Clarion*, 25 May 1934.
33. Hansard, 3 July, 1930, vol. 240 cc2131–2.
34. *Clarion*, 25 May 1934.
35. Ellen Wilkinson, 'The Red Trade Union Congress', *The Communist,* 17 September 1921.
36. *The Labour Monthly*, Sept 1921, p. 218.
37. *The Communist*, 27 August 1921.
38. 'The Women's Movement in Soviet Russia', *The Communist Review*, No.1 Vol. 2, November 1921, pp. 26–9.
39. *Ibid.*, p. 29.
40. See June Hannam and Karen Hunt, *Socialist Women*, Routledge, 2002, p. 186.
41. *Ibid.*
42. Report of the International Congress of Women, Zurich, 12–17 May 1919, p. 78.
43. *Ibid.*, p. 181.
44. Report of the National Conference of Women, 15 and 16 October 1918, p. 88.
45. *The New Dawn*, April 1923.
46. American Commission on Conditions in Ireland, 23 March 1921, pp. 623, 5th Report, Nation (New York) Vol. 112, No. 2907 section 11.
47. *Labour Woman*, 1 January 1926, p. 2.
48. Report on Revolutionary Organisations in the United Kingdom, 15 November 1923.
49. *Ibid.*, 17 February 1921.

50. *Ibid.*, April 1922, p. 19.
51. National Easter Delegate Meeting, March 1921.
52. *All Power,* December 1922, p. 6.
53. *The New Dawn*, 15 September 1923.
54. *Ibid.*, April 1923.
55. Wright Robinson, 1923, MRO, pp. 131–6.
56. *Ibid.*
57. *Ashton-Under-Lyne Reporter*, 24 November 1923, p. 9.
58. *Daily Mail*, 18 September 1923.
59. *Ashton-under-Lyne Reporter*, 1 December 1923, p. 5.
60. Stella Davies, *North Country Born*, Routledge and Kegan Paul, 1963, p. 70.
61. Letter to Rajani Palme Dutt, August 1923, PHM.
62. *Ibid.*, 27 June 1924.
63. *Westminster Gazette*, 22 February 1923.
64. *All Power*, September 1922, p. 6.

Chapter 3

1. Ellen Picton-Turberville MP, *Windsor Magazine*, March 1931.
2. Nancy Astor, *Evening News*, 12 February 1925.
3. *John Bull*, 30 January 1932.
4. At the time, Ellen was a strict vegetarian. She campaigned against fox hunting and deer hunting, helped found the New League against cruel sports and persuaded the Kitchen Committee at the House of Commons to provide at least one vegetarian dish a day at the House of Commons. However, by the 1930s she was no longer a vegetarian – indeed she had paintings of bull fights on her wall.
5. *The New Dawn*, 20 June 1925, p. 8.
6. *Ibid.*, 21 July 1928, p. 354.
7. Letter to Nancy Astor, undated but posted 29 January 1929, Nancy Astor archives.
8. *Hansard*, 11 November 1926.
9. *Ibid.*, 1 December 1926.
10. Letter from Nancy Astor to Eleanor Rathbone, 24 November 1927.
11. *Reynolds*, 17 May 1925.
12. *Birmingham Sunday Mercury*, 29 March 1925.
13. *Hansard*, 10 March 1926.
14. Bondfield and Lawrence were both re-elected in by-elections in 1926.
15. Letter to Nancy Astor, 5 March 1929.

16. *Hansard*, 28 November 1930.

17. *Ibid.*, 9 November 1927.

18. *The Labour Woman*, 1 July 1924.

19. Labour Party conference, 1925; 1926.

20. *Hansard*, 9 February 1926.

21. Quoted in Clare Debenham, *'Grassroots Feminism': A Study of the Campaign of the Society for the Provision of Birth Control Clinics, 1924–1938*, PhD, University of Manchester, 2010, p. 187.

22. *Ibid.*

23. Deputation to Clynes from the SJO, 12 December 1929, PHM.

24. National conference of Labour Women, 23–25 April 1929, p. 31.

25. *Hansard*, 5 May 1925.

26. *Nottingham Evening Post*, 31 May 1926, p. 1.

27. *Lansbury's Labour Weekly*, 5 June 1926, p. 7.

28. *Hansard*, 29 June 1926.

29. Labour Party report of the 26th annual conference, 11–15 October 1926, p. 243.

30. *The New Dawn*, 16 March 1929, p. 139.

31. *Ibid.*, 16 April 1927, p. 182.

32. Letter to Dutt, 12 November 1927, PHM.

33. *Ibid.*

34. Labour Party conference, 3 October 1927, p. 183.

Chapter 4

1.   Thank-you letter to Leonard Elmhurst, undated but circa 1929.

2.   Beatrice Webb's *Diaries*, May 1929. Webb was referring to Margaret Bondfield.

3.   *Hansard*, 21 March 1930.

4.   Letter to Leonard Elmhirst, 26 September 1931.

5.   *Hansard*, 5 February 1930.

6.   *Ibid.*, 5 November 1930.

7.   *The New Dawn* , 2 August 1930, p. 382.

8.   *Hansard*, 15 July 1931.

9.   28 September 1931, unpublished note.

10. Letter to Leonard Elmhirst, 9 October 1931.

11. *Daily Express*, 16 February 1932, p. 9.

12. *Ibid.*, 30 October 1931, p. 10.

13. *The New Dawn*, 7 November 1931, p. 554.

14. *Daily Express*, 18 February 1932, p. 9.
15. Winifred Holtby, 17 September, 1934, L WH/6/6.1/15/08C.
16. Ellen Wilkinson to Winifred Holtby, circa 1933, L WH/3/3/27/034.
17. *Ibid.*
18. *Ibid.*, circa 1934.
19. *Daily Express*, 8 May 1933, p. 10.
20. National conference of Labour Women, 14–16 June 1932, pp. 56–7.
21. *Ibid.*, pp. 89–90.
22. *Ibid.*, 23–25 May 1933, p. 58.
23. *Daily Express*, 18 April 1932, p. 10.
24. *Ibid.*, 3 October 1933, p. 1.
25. *Ibid.*, 2 October 1934, p. 10.
26. Labour Party conference, 1934, p. 221.
27. *Ibid.*
28. Letter to Winifred Holtby, circa 1934.
29. *Daily Express*, 18 January 1934, pp. 1–2.
30. Ellen Wilkinson to Winifred Holtby, circa 1933, L WH/3/3/27/034, p. 195.

Chapter 5

1. Ellen Wilkinson and Edward Conze, *Why Fascism?*, Selwyn and Blount, 1934, p. 9.
2. Frederick Voight, the *Guardian*'s German correspondent, to Ellen Wilkinson, PHM.
3. Ellen Wilkinson's Visit to Germany, unpublished manuscript, July 1932, PHM.
4. Winifred Holtby to Lady Rhondda, Wednesday, 6 September 1933, L WH/5/5/24/04/05a, Hull.
5. Foreign Office, 9 September 1933, FO 371/16755.
6. Letter from F.A. Newsam to G.A. Mounsey, 27 November 1933, FO 371/16755. The actual reports are missing and were probably destroyed.
7. NEC Minutes, 30 August 1934, p. 124.
8. Labour Party conference, 1933, p. 221.
9. *Daily Express*, 23 February 1934, p. 10.
10. Labour Party conference, 1934, p. 186–7.
11. *Feed the Children*, Committee for the Relief of Victims of German Fascism, 1933, p. 9.
12. Hugh Dalton, *The Fateful Years: Memoirs, 1931–1945*, Muller, 1957, p. 108.
13. See *Hansard*, 14 March 1938, vol. 33, cc45–169.

14. *Hansard*, 24 August 1939.
15. AUCE Annual Delegate Meeting, 1938, p. 43.
16. See http://tinyurl.com/psvzo9h.
17. *Guardian*, 24 November 1934, p. 20.
18. Ernest Robinson to Middleton, 17 November 1934.
19. NEC Manifesto, 28 April 1937.
20. Comments on Special Branch Report, June 1937.
21. Draft circular, Spain Campaign Committee, November 1937.
22. C.R. Atlee, Ellen Wilkinson, Philip Noel Baker and John Dugdale, *We Saw in Spain*, Labour Party, 1937.
23. Spain Campaign Committee Minutes, 31 March 1938, p. 2.
24. Memorandum to the Executive, May 1938.
25. *Hansard*, 28 July 1938.
26. Labour Party conference report, Southport, May 1939, pp. 256–7.
27. *The World of Labour*, March 1927.
28. *Time and Tide*, 30 April 1932.
29. Imprisoned for organising a rail strike.
30. *Hansard*, 29 June 1936.
31. *Daily Telegraph*, 10 October 1934.
32. Ellen Wilkinson et al., *Condition of India – Being the Report of the Delegation sent to India by the India League in 1932*, Essential News, 1932, p. 507.
33. *Guardian*, 8 March 1938, p. 12.

Chapter 6

1. Ellen Wilkinson, *The Town that was Murdered*, Gollancz, 1939, pp. 191–2.
2. *Ibid.*, p. 220.
3. *John Bull*, 1 January 1938, p. 9.
4. *The Times*, 26 October 1936, p. 15.
5. Four councillors marched all the way, the mayor dropped in intermittently and the rest only joined the march at the last stage.
6. *Observer*, 25 October 1936, p. 33.
7. Labour Party report of the 36th annual conference 5–9 October 1936.
8. Wilkinson, *The Town that was Murdered*, p. 204.
9. *The Times*, 2 November 1936, p. 11.
10. Cabinet minutes 56 (36) p. 244.
11. *The Times*, 27 October, p. 11.
12. *Ibid.*, 31 October, p. 9.
13. *Guardian*, 2 November 1936, p. 14.

14. Wilkinson, *The Town that was Murdered*, p. 208.
15. Cabinet minutes.
16. Undated newspaper cutting, Durham Public Library.
17. Malcolm Pearce and Geoffrey Stewart, *British Political History, 1867–2001*, Routledge, 1992, p. 359.
18. Wilkinson, *The Town that was Murdered*, p. 210.
19. *Labour Woman*, May 1936, p. 71.
20. *Daily Express*, 7 October 1937, p. 7.
21. See Chapter 5.
22. *Ibid.*, 26 January 1939.
23. AUCE Annual Delegate Meeting, 1939.
24. *Guardian*, 21 December 1961, p. 6.
25. See Peter Scott's, 'The Twilight World of Inter-War British Hire Purchase' *Past and Present* November, 2002 pp. 195–225 for an analysis of this.
26. *The Times*, 11 December 1937, p. 14.
27. *Ibid.*, 7 May 1938, p. 12.
28. In 1948, after 34 years of campaigning, women were eventually granted the right to their own nationality regardless of marital status.
29. Beatrice Webb Diary, 28 July 1931.
30. *Ibid.*, 2 September 1935.
31. *Hansard*, 17 February 1938.
32. *Ibid.*, 22 February 1937.

Chapter 7

1. AUCE Annual Delegate Meeting, 1941, p. 10.
2. NEC Minutes, 10 May 1942, p. 2.
3. Ellen Wilkinson, *Plan For Peace*, 1944.
4. *Daily Express*, 11 October 1940, p. 6.
5. *Guardian*, 12 June 1941, p. 2.
6. *Guardian*, 28 February 1941, p. 5.
7. *Nottingham Evening Post*, 15 October 1940, p. 4.
8. *Midlands Daily Telegraph*, 20 September 1941.
9. *Ibid.*, 10 October 1941.
10. Tube Shelter Enquiry, April, 1943.
11. Wright Robinson diary, 13 April 1942.
12. *The Times*, 22 January 1943, p. 2.
13. *Tamworth Herald* 30 October 1943, p. 4.
14. *The New Dawn*, 15 March 1941, p. 82.

15. In May 1941 the Commons Chamber burnt down because MPs did not do their fire-watching duties.
16. *Coventry Evening Telegraph*, 23 October 1942.
17. *Manchester Guardian*, 5 October 1942.
18. *Coventry Evening Telegraph*, 5 October 1942.
19. *Ibid.*, 10 October 1942.
20. *Birmingham Gazette*, 5 November 1942.
21. *Coventry Evening Telegraph*, 5 October 1942.
22. AUCE annual delegate meeting, 1943, p. 32.
23. *The Times*, 18 October 1944, p. 2.
24. *Guardian*, 25 August 1941, p. 3.
25. Annual delegate meeting, 1942.
26. *Leader*, 3 March 1945, p. 11.
27. Tom Driberg, *Leader*, 3 March 1945, p. 11.
28. *Daily Mirror*, 16 April 1945.
29. NEC minutes, 28 March 1945, p. 22.

Chapter 8

1. Policy Committee, Points for Discussion, September 1944.
2. Labour Party Research Programme, October 1946.
3. Michael Young, 1990 interview, British Library.
4. *Let us Face the Future*, 1945, p. 3.
5. NEC minutes, 29 October 1944.
6. *The New Dawn*, 6 June 1945, p. 178.
7. Labour Party conference, May 1945, p. 152.
8. *The New Dawn*, 16 June 1945, p. 178.
9. Obituary, Labour Party conference, 1947.
10. Hugh Dalton, *The Fateful Years: Memoirs, 1931–1945*, Muller, 1957, p. 222.
11. *Ibid.*, p. 223.
12. *The New Dawn*, 20 October 1945, p. 330.
13. Interview with Leah Manning in Donoughue Bernard and G.W. Jones, *Herbert Morrison, Portrait of a Politician*, Phoenix Press, 2001, p. 346.
14. *Ibid.*
15. *Guardian*, 9 February 1947, p. 7.
16. Attlee papers, 18 May–13 August 1945, dep. 18, fols. 67–81.
17. See WHN blog March 7 2011.
18. I am indebted to Robert Pearce for this insight.

19. Letter to Morgan Phillips, 12 March 1946, PHM. I am grateful to Darren Tredwell for this reference.
20. Letter from Tawney, 30 September 1945, Attlee dep. 23.
21. Ellen Wilkinson to Harold Laski, 3 June 1946.
22. Susan Lawrence, *Fabian Quarterly*, March 1947.
23. Labour Party conference, 1946, p. 189.
24. Mr Cove, Hansard, 22 March 1946.
25. Jean Mann, *Woman in Parliament*, Odhams, 1962, pp. 39–40.
26. PRO ED 136/727.
27. Labour Party conference 1946.
28. *Ibid.*, p. 191.
29. *Guardian*, 2 July 1946, p. 6.
30. Joint Memorandum by the Minister of Education and Secretary of State for Scotland, 21 February 1946.
31. *Daily Telegraph*, 14 June 1945.
32. Apparently Thatcher spoke against it.
33. Visit to Germany, 2–6 October 1945, Secret Report by the Minister of Education.
34. *Ibid.*
35. *Ibid.*
36. Letters between Wilkinson and Attlee, 17 September, 9 October 1945.

Conclusion

1. *Time and Tide*, 15 February 1947. I am grateful to Angela V. John for this reference.
2. Interview with Leah Manning in Donoughue Bernard and G.W. Jones, *Herbert Morrison, Portrait of a Politician*, Phoenix Press, 2001, p. 392.
3. NEC minutes, 26 February 1947. Bessie Braddock replaced her.
4. *Manchester Guardian*, 7 February 1947.
5. In May 1931, Ellen presented a Bill to allow 'the right of access to mountains and moorlands'. The Bill failed. The Right to Roam was not granted until March 1999.
6. Ellen Wilkinson and Edward Conze, *Why Fascism?*, Selwyn and Blount, circa 1930s, p. 240.
7. Interview with Zoe Williams, *Guardian*, 11 February 2012.
8. I am grateful to Teréz Kleisz for this information.
9. *The New Dawn*, 11 December 1926, p. 11.

Index